MONOGRAPH 68

INTERNATIONAL ECONOMIC DISORDER
&
A GANDHIAN SOLUTION

International Economic Disorder
(A THEORY OF ECONOMIC DARWINISM)
&
A Gandhian Solution

J.D. SETHI

Member, Planning Commission

INDIAN INSTITUTE OF ADVANCED STUDY, SHIMLA
in collaboration with
VIKAS PUBLISHING HOUSE PVT. LTD., NEW DELHI

337
S49i

First published 1990

© Indian Institute of Advanced Study, Shimla

Published by
The Secretary (A&F)
Indian Institute of Advanced Study
Rashtrapati Nivas, Shimla
in association with
Vikas Publishing House Pvt. Ltd.
576 Masjid Road, Jangpura Extension, New Delhi

ISBN 0-7069-5441-6

Typeset at Tulika Print Communication Services Pvt. Ltd.
15/15 Sarvapriya Vihar, New Delhi 110 016

Printed at Rajbandhu Industrial Company
C-61 Mayapuri Phase II, New Delhi

TO
MY RESPECTED FRIEND
MORARJI DESAI

FOREWORD

The essential argument of this monograph by Professor J.D. Sethi is worth underlining at the outset. In the international economic order today, the rich are becoming richer and the poor are becoming poorer as groups, classes, countries and nations. The latter are generally referred to as the LDCs, the Third World or the South.

There are basically two sets of theories which attempt to describe the international economic order: the dependency theories and the theories of interdependence. Both of these rationalize, and by implication justify, the prevailing order, concealing the essential fact of Darwinism in which the strong economies are flourishing at the cost of the weak, leading essentially to economic ruptures. That is why the author prefers to use the epithet 'disorder' rather than 'order' for the international economic relationships. The author strongly argues that South has not yet perceived two serious threats from the North. First, unlike before, the ADCs have decided to push the South from global decision-making. Second, unless the nations of South cooperate among themselves more seriously, the idea of North-South dialogue will always remain a non-starter. The only solution to this global problem, in his view, lies in a Gandhian approach to the global economy.

This view is most likely to provoke discussion, and that is one purpose of its publication.

J.S. GREWAL

CONTENTS

INTRODUCTION

I

Typologies or classifications of the prevailing global system, based on one theory or the other, are bewilderingly complex and unamenable to comprehension by the common man. The global system itself remains imprecisely defined. Broadly it means the whole structure of nation-states, international institutions, processes and relations that influence or determine the behaviour and fate of people and states. We cannot be concerned with all these, no matter in what order they are organized. Besides the superpowers, there are a dozen or so middle powers who do not interact with one another as middle powers in any significant way. Then there are a large number of nations, small powers, which are victims of aggression, exploitation and blackmail. Some of these may have extraordinary leverage. However, as a total subset, the small powers wield much less influence than they can if only they were united.

Big powers are dangerous and yet are self-proclaimed preservers of peace and guarantors as well as beneficiaries of the global order. Probably the most significant aspect of the global system is the total domination of it by *international regimes*. The decline of the UN and attempts to create supernational agencies encompassing the whole world have given birth to these regimes. They are military, political, ideological and economic in nature. The NATO and WARSAW are military regimes; the EEC, ASEAN, SAARC, GFC and OAU are economic regimes; and the Islamic Bloc, Arab League, NAM and CHOGAM are political regimes.

Various models of the world order are being suggested for the future but almost all of them are extensions of a set of analytical theories and ideologies based on a single paradigm, be it capitalist, socialist or any other, and aim at the survival of the existing international world economy, which is of marginal significance for the welfare of the majority of the people. Even where the models or their typologies have strong explanatory powers, they are not necessarily valid or relevant for having an equitable order. This is because one man's, or nation's order is another's disorder. The extermination of the Jews by the Nazis was a highly ordered and structured business. There is, thus, no common conception of 'world order'.

In Gilpin's 'three models of the future', the first set of models rests on the distinctions between liberalism, marxism and nationalism. The distinctions are very blurred now, if not irrelevant. The second set has the *sovereignty-at-by* model, the dependency model and the mercantalist model, in which one or more big economic powers are allowed to combine regionalism with economic dominance.[1]

The third is a choice among (i) natural–rational; (ii) positivist–evolutionary, and (iii) historical–dialectical. According to (i), liberal pluralism, which exists in many countries, must be extended to satisfy the conditions for a just world order.[2] But the prevailing order is not an embodiment of the unified family of man. The positivist–evolutionary political science argues that authoritarianism is the characteristic of early stages of political development and legitimizes manipulation of 'pluralism' in poor countries by powerful external, political and economic forces. The positivist–evolutionary view has two main currents: functionalism (i.e., federalism or transnational arrangement), and the notion of a global ecological system, both taking as given the existing structure of power and social relations from which future trends can be extrapolated. The historico–dialectical approach claims the possibility of understanding changes in the basic structure of power and social relations by searching out sequences or points of conflict and the conception of a new emerging world order. But history is no guide for such an order, even though dialectics remain valid. The reason is that the crucial battleground between equilibrium and dialectical analyses remains unchanged. It is not history that repeats itself; it is the historians who do so.

The fourth, one version of the dialectical model with its historical trappings blown over, is the dependency centre-periphery

[1] R. Gilpin, 'Three Models of the Future', *International Organization*, Winter 1975.

[2] R.W. Cox, 'On Thinking about Future World Order', *World Politics*, January 1976.

model which has a powerful explanatory quality but little by way of solutions. If the dependency theory itself has been marginalized, it is not surprising. Indeed, it can be linked with the second set of models mentioned above.

However, in view of the widespread use of violence, a rather cranky version of the model—the guerrilla-terrorist actions of a nation—extends itself to an international situation. It accepts the prevailing conceptualization of bipolarity and multipolarity. The model is the creation of a system by simply subdividing the bipolar and multipolar universes according to the power of guerrilla-terrorist actions and now by the rise of new fundamentalism.[3] At best, the model is a plea for reconciliation of favoured structural characterization with the increasing influences of non-state groups. At an international plane, it divides the world between a few big powers and the rest. This is the extreme model for status quo despite appearing to be radical. This is because it legitimizes state violence, a million times more powerful, in order to legitimize its own guerrilla violence. Consequently, poverty and political repression, like evil and disaster, are very ordinary now.

The fifth set of models are the most popular and are best summed up in the Brandt Report. The Chenry model, the Prebrisch model, various UN models and even their corrective critiques, whether real or apparent, are taken care of in the Brandt model.[4] According to these models: (i) The world is in a state of disequilibrium, amplified by new scarcities in raw materials, food crisis in poor countries, oil crisis, global inflation and unemployment, international financial instability. (ii) The world can be divided into four groupings—advanced capitalist countries, communist countries, developing countries, and countries whose prospects for development are not bright. The last mentioned countries are called the fourth world, the others being the first, second and third worlds, in that order. (iii) These politico-economic groupings can evolve an arrangement for cooperation and coordination for the benefit of all at the same time. It is possible to arrange the prevailing order into a general positive-sum game relations. A more 'humane' version of it is Galtury's projection of Japanese society and economy to the world system which gives the idea of peace as a kind of harmony

[3] L.R. Beres, 'Guerrillas, Terrorists and Polarity: New Structural Models of World Politics', *Western Political Quarterly*, December 1974.

[4] *North South: A Programme for Survival*, Pan Books, London, 1980.

where smaller and weaker nations are guided by big and strong nations.[5]

For the poor nations all the aforementioned models are only of academic interest. At best they conform to the complex realities of the prevailing world order only partially. These typologies conceal the real interests of the dominant groups who are pitted against others living in poverty, illiteracy and squalor. There are rich nations and poor nations but the world order divided into nation-states also conceals the alliance between the ruling classes or elites of most nation-states, which leaves at least two billion people in the cold. Few radicals can remove their ideological blinkers to see this grand alliance. Cardose saw this relationship clearly when he wrote about the relationship between national and international forces as forming a 'complex whole whose structural links are not based on mere external forms of exploitation and coercion, but are rooted in coincidence of interests between local dominant classes and international ones and, on the other side, are challenged by local dominated groups and classes'.[6]

That is why the distinction between North and South—a divide between the privileged and the underprivileged—is of much greater significance. The latter are increasingly pushed out of global decision-making, with a few crumbs and weapons thrown for their consumption. Corresponding to natural or social Darwinism, there is an International Economic Darwinism. All the North-South conferences have ended in a stalemate, increased distrust, bitterness and pervasive cynicism. This is the principal contradiction of the world order and not that between great powers. *This is also the central focus of this book.*

Yet, in another way, this global order is moving towards greater stability in the wake of the US-Soviet detente, and Eastern Europe's dismantling of authoritarian regimes and its desire to integrate itself with the advanced capitalist world. However, this thrust towards stability is bypassing the third world which is moving in the opposite direction, i.e., towards new instability that is reflected in stagnant growth, poverty and illiteracy, a declining share in global trade and technology, and a plethora of social unrest and violence bordering on civil war. The advanced developed countries (ADCs), both capitalist and communist, notwithstanding their

[5] J. Galtury, 'Japan and Future World Politics', *Journal of Peace Research*, 1973.

[6] F.H. Cardose and E. Faletto, *Dependence and Development in Latin America*, University of California, Berkeley, 1979, p. xvi.

massive weapon concentration, are dividing the world into two halves, the ADCs and the LDCs (Less Developed Countries). Within this global divide, there is a variety of subdivisions but none so powerful as to challenge this divide. A nation's position on one scale determines its position on all other scales.

No matter which classification one prefers, there is no escape from the ugly fact that a vast majority of nations of the third and fourth worlds are pushed or have pushed themselves into a dangerous situation of international ghettos or of forced Darwinism. Notwithstanding all the models and theories, they face utter hopelessness on account of big power hegemony and their capacity to externalize their problems or on account of their own self-inflicted wounds.

The volcanic changes that have taken place in Eastern Europe and are forcing on them a shift from socialism to market economies, as well as the changes that are taking place in Latin America, suggest that the rest of the LDCs would be deprived of the global resources earmarked for their development. Already the US Congress and administration have sent ample warnings in this direction. The idea of one Europe would mean further integration of the ADCs and larger investment of EEC resources in East European countries. This is a new threat to the survival of the LDCs.

President George Bush, in his national security message of Congress given in the third week of March 1990, indicated that the USA would pay special attention to pre-positioning equipment and supplies in countries in the third world which shared strategic perceptions. Ironically, President Bush now sees danger from the third world. While recognizing the need for vigilance against the Soviet Union, he emphasized the importance of having an adequate and appropriate United States force to deal with third world conflicts or threats which endanger American security.[7]

II

Economic Darwinism is both a new form of international order and a threat to the poor nations. What we call Darwinism is nearer to Galbraith's 'Second Imperialism' which deals with the core nations' behaviour vis-à-vis others. The will to national independence, according to him, is the most powerful force in modern times. Therefore, its antithesis is not mere imperialism but, to use Kaut-

[7] *Tribune*, March 22, 1990.

sky's phrase, 'Ultra Imperialism'. If the national leadership is strong, effective and well regarded, it will not tolerate foreign domination. If the leadership is weak, ineffective, unpopular, corrupt and oppressive, it may accept foreign guidance, support and a measure of domination, to be ultimately marginalized. But then it may not be tolerated by its own people. This is the eroding effect of new imperialism.[8] On the one hand, it reduces the need for conflict between imperial powers and gives them a chance for deeper cooperation, and, on the other, provides them the opportunity for deeper penetration or total neglect of the LDCs. The last one is called Darwinism.

It may be of some interest to the reader that the concept of Economic Darwinism has found renewed interest in the history of economic thought. For instance, Veblen's theory of economic behaviour is characterized as Darwinism. Veblen judged all classical and neoclassical (orthodox) static equilibrium theory to be pre-Darwinian, old-fashioned and outmoded. Others have characterized as Darwinian, Adam Smith's 'theories of competition and the division of labour that led to the development of speciation and natural selection. Heretofore it has been thought that Malthus was the source of Darwin's evolutionary concepts.'[9]

Attempts to slur over the historical background of the LDCs, as to how they arrived at the present position, have blurred the analytical perspective. It is not necessary to get into the old arid debate about historicism, or whether the use of the dialectical rather than the equilibrium model of analysis is more relevant, or to establish the superiority of one model over another. What is required is to determine the effect of the international system on national situations by which the LDCs are being pushed out of history as unnecessary objects.

To understand the problem better, we have to shift the emphasis from an analytical analysis to a historical one. Under old imperialism and colonialism, there was a much greater degree of integration between the North and the South and also much more explicit exploitation. In the post-independence phase, there seemed to be an unprecedented push towards greater international cooperation among the ADCs only. However, attempts were made to restruc-

    [8] John Kenneth Galbraith, 'The Second Imperial Regimism', *International Security*, Winter 1982–83.
    [9] For discussion see, R.W. Ault and R.E. Ekelund, 'Habits in Economic Analysis', *History of Political Economy*, Fall 1988.

ture the old relationship in two ways: (i) by starting the system of semi-colonial modernization as fast as possible under conditions of political independence and (ii) by so concentrating on the development of the North as to make it more autonomous, and thus leaving the South to its own devices. The crude fact is that the ruling elites of the LDCs joined with the nations of the ADCs in order to profit from these two developments while leaving the people of the South to fend for themselves, without realizing that they are being alienated from their own people.

Thus, we see a series of paradoxes. While attempts are made to maintain colonial exploitation in new forms at whatever level it is feasible, the LDCs and ADCs are drifting away from one another into two different worlds. The structural changes and growth patterns of the latter make them more and more autonomous from the economies of the former which are slow to bring about structural changes, to have growth and social justice. The word rupture means the growing autonomy of the ADCs vis-à-vis LDCs, less of interdependence. The paradox is that the more the world is 'integrated', the greater is the rupture between one set of nations and the other.

We may find all this in the linkages of trade, technology, ecology and growth. The essentials of the theory of trade are: (i) comparative advantage; (ii) free trade and specialization in products bring about factor free equalization; (iii) trade promotes development in the form of higher consumption and production. These arguments which started with David Ricardo, have wrought havoc. In a world of changing technologies, capital accumulation, economies of scale and imperialism, trade has produced results contrary to expectations for the LDCs. Labour is confined to low productivity areas (nation-state barriers) and capital to high productivity areas (no barriers). Kitamura proved that international trade, if not assisted by the consciously guided transfers of factors of production, has no inherent tendency to equalize incomes and productivity levels. Indeed, the trade mechanism works the other way round, in favour of the progressive countries and against stagnant ones.[10]

In the area of ecology and technology, Lester R. Brown in his 1985 Worldwatch Report has given statistics to prove that the emergence of a highly developed internal economy provides a way of trans-

---

[10] H. Kitamura, 'Capital Accumulation and the Theory of International Trade', *Malaysian Economic Review*, Vol. 3, No. 1.

mitting scarcities from one country to another, a sort of domino theory of ecological stress and collapse. Soil erosion, for example, has historically been a local problem; civilizations whose food systems were undermined by erosion, in times past, declined in isolation. But in the integrated world economy of the late twentieth century, food—like oil—is a global commodity. A country that loses an excessive amount of topsoil needs to import more food and thereby raises the pressure on soils elsewhere.[11]

The entire international economic establishment, which includes the developed world, international financial institutions, the UN system, the economic *gurus*, and the third world elite, was tied to the growth rate of the developed world. Statistical correlations were worked out to prove the point. But all theories of growth, ranging from trickle-down to basic needs accompaniments, marked the great deception as they all legitimized Darwinism. Third world growth slumped badly and its growth rate did not pick up after 1973 through the cycles of growth of the developed world.

It is universally recognized that the present international system is in some kind of crisis. Capitalism is in crisis, communism is in crisis, the third world is in crisis, and so on. But talking about crises has become an international industry. Those who control the international system or its sub-system and who enjoy its fruits, living in great luxury, are most vocal about it. One of the techniques they have developed is to talk continuously about the urgency to help the poor. International organizations such as the UN, NAM and the Commonwealth produce mountains of documents. This exercise creates the illusion that somebody is concerned about the world and its people. In reality, this is a fraudulent exercise.

Since this exercise is conducted through top world leaders of the great powers, it becomes difficult to expose its real meanings in order to understand what is really happening behind the scene, and why the present highly exploitative and inequitous international order as well as national orders are continuing.

No matter how one looks at its opponents or critics, the system is nothing but a well-designed international dictatorship: political, economic and military. International economic monopolies buttress this dictatorship. Paradoxically this dictatorship is internally democratic and externally authoritarian. The two superpowers which seem to be engaged in many serious conflicts, a nuclear

---

[11] *State of the World*, 1985, p. 7.

weapons race, and attempts to collect friends, allies and bases, are really engaged in re-arranging the world so that both can keep their dominance over the rest of the world through an artificially created unstable competition. No matter how fierce the competition, and now detente, between them over weapons, resources and control of areas, all this is within the recognized new rules of ADCs' global integration. The so-called New International Economic order has proved to be a historical equivalent to the end of a development ideology of economic and social justice.

Global reordering requires a firm and clear understanding of the prevailing order and, more significantly, of what is so wrong with it that it needs fundamental rather than incremental change. Is there a common plot with a limited number of endings, asks Mary Kaldor, without giving an answer. She can't give an answer because she and other left liberals, along with others from the west, belong to the intellectual club of international Darwinists.

The LDCs have, both by choice and compulsion, opted for a long-drawn journey towards individual and collective suicide. No matter what politics its member nations pursue on the basis of the present and proposed world order model, suicide is ensured unless they get out of Darwinism by (i) downgrading trade, (ii) changing domestic development strategies, (iii) inter-LDC cooperation; and finally (iv) by changing their own ruling elites who are junior partners of the international Darwinists.

III

The present study is concerned with the central question: which way is the world economic order moving, with what prospects for the LDCs, and what value can be placed on various development strategies? Even more critical is the question of international constraints imposed on domestic strategies. No effort is made to evaluate the variety of analytical perspectives or models mentioned earlier as the material circumstances and power economic interests negate all rational but mutually exclusive perspectives. Indeed, the crucial question is why the third world disaster?

Paradoxically all economic theories survive with varying acceptability. Neo-classical, Keynesian, Marxian, Dependency, Interdependence because all have been found to rest on a single paradigm. Even those who recognized that disengagement from the international economy had strong logical grounds got scared for fear of suggesting a defeatist solution. Even the radicals who took a bold stand by asking, could the inflow of foreign capital stunt what might otherwise be vigorous local development of the so-called scarce factors of production, went completely silent. The world power contenders have key agents among radicals as well as among conservatives in the LDCs whom they have institutionalized in their own framework.

It seems impossible that any set of reforms of the existing system, with its structural characteristics kept intact, can improve the situation for the South or the poverty-ridden people of the third world. Some countries may benefit from reforms, but by and large what goes under the general demand of a New International Economic Order is either impossible to achieve or irrelevant for the poor of the South. Therefore, an alternative approach or response to the prevailing situation, which is characterized by Darwinism, has become absolutely necessary. It is futile to suggest abstract models. It is even more important that no institution should be demolished unless an alternative institution can replace it. Therefore, in our view, the only alternative approach can be Gandhian. It will press for such reforms of the existing system as make its replacement smoother and easier and with minimum damage.

There can be four primary thrusts in the Gandhian response to the prevailing crisis. First, in view of the exploitative character of the local order in which for the first time exploitation is taking the shape of violent structural dualism, rupture or the ghetto syndrome, the LDCs will have to avoid integration with this system dominated by the big powers, their multinationals and technologies which further divide the world. The LDCs will have to demystify such concepts as interdependence, one-world model, or mutually reinforcing growth, which cover up underlying dualisms. The more they try to integrate with this world, the more brusquely they will be pushed out. Therefore, they have to adopt a strategy of first *detaching themselves from the system and then reattaching with it* when their economic position is less vulnerable.

Second, excessive reliance on trade, foreign aid and investment, import of technologies relevant to ADCs and on the economic theories of the west will have to be given up. This approach would certainly cost high initially and even mean some disruption of inessential sectors, but in the long run it would give a push to greater self-reliance. To minimize the damage of giving low priority to trade, aid and foreign investment, it would be necessary for the countries of the third world to enter into mutual cooperation in a wide variety of areas. The South has to treat itself not merely as an entity but as a developing mode of production outside the ADC system. It is seldom realized that the prevalent LDC-ADC cooperation on an individual basis militates against South-South cooperation. The power rests in mercantalist absolutism in the garb of GATT, etc. For instance, multinationals restrict the area of export from one developing country to another. For genuine South-South cooperation all multinationals which impose such restrictions will have to be blacked out. Gandhi's theory of dumping of low-grade industries from the ADCs into LDCs has proved to be absolutely correct.

Third, and the most important Gandhian response, would be an absolute reversal of the existing strategy of growth and development being pursued by the LDCs. Almost all the models of growth and development currently in operation are western-oriented, be they capitalist or Marxist or some combination of the two. All the western models are based on a single paradigm in which capital accumulation, incremental capital-output ratio, and capital-labour ratio are designed to save labour rather than capital. This paradigm has to be rejected and replaced by one in which human and natural resource development, employment maximization and production by masses, instead of mass production of goods, become the central features.

Fourth, there is a deep relationship between the economic, political and cultural processes. In most LDCs, authoritarianism, poverty and cultural dependency have gone together. India may seem to be an exception but it is not so. Her cultural dependency is legitimized by the so-called democratically elected elite. A Gandhian would begin by demonstrating cultural resistance to the ADCs approach because therein lie the roots of elite consumption, poverty and massive state repression.

However, the main focus of this essay remains on International Economic Darwinism which holds out no hope for the LDCs. An international revolution has to begin by organizing the people of the South to eliminate Darwinism and global disorder, the latter defined as imperialism, colonialism and cultural domination, interdependence, or whatever.

THE SOUTH AND ECONOMIC DARWINISM

I

The global economic system has marginalized the third world, to some extent by exploiting it and more so now by pushing it out of the global decision-making system. Except for those nations which have struggled to come up to become middle income countries or newly industrialized countries (NICs), all others are being treated as international ghettos. In this situation the ruling elites of the third world are openly accepting the job of undermining their own economies and societies, though of course at a price. The most critical crisis in the third world, therefore, seems to be that it is its lot to remain in poverty and squalor for ever.

All the theories and models of the global system that have been put forward, have one thing in common: they either assume some kind of integration between nations or minimize the problems of structural ruptures. As solutions to problems or changes from one order to another are predicated upon certain assumptions, the rejection of integration or interdependence will produce solutions quite the opposite to those which its acceptance will produce. None of the models of order or disorder seem to expose the rupturing of disintegrating forces which are imposing upon us a new classification. Models are spread over from the extreme right to the extreme left. For instance, there is the dependency theory on the extreme left and the theory of full market interdependence on the extreme right. In between there are other theories that tilt to one side or the other, or which are a combination of the two, such as the Brandt Commission and the Prebisch-Singer models. All have their strong points but each one is so partial in its analysis as to botch the perspective.

Ironically, the more left wing the analysis the less policy options it can recommend, and the more rightist the analysis the greater the support it derives from current policy making. This is because the prevailing order suits both the advanced developed countries (ADCs), whether capitalist or communist, and the ruling elites of the less developed countries (LDCs).

Probably the most serious crisis today is one of *economic rupture* between nations as well as between people which, for want of a better title, I christen as International Economic Darwinism (IED), hereafter called International Darwinism or Economic Darwinism.

The meaning and scope of IED lie in its explanation which is given in what follows. At this stage a summary definition will do. IED is a global theory of economic and some non-economic relations among nations (nation-states) or among peoples of nations, in which one set is not only exploited but is being pushed away by the other, or is so marginalized that it is almost out of global decision-making, making its survival of no more consequence than a ghetto's.

Almost all theories of trade are based on certain assumptions which have never been fully valid and have certainly declined in their value and validity in recent years. Four assumptions deserve special mention. First, that the global economy is one unified whole and trade is the most important unifying factor. It will be shown here that trade has, in fact, become an instrument of fracturing the global economy. Second, some trade is better than no trade. It can be shown and has been shown that even if there are certain competitive advantages over a wide range of goods, trade may be injurious for other reasons. Third, the principle of the international division of labour, which was derived from the general principles of division of labour as propounded by Adam Smith and elaborated by Karl Marx, is one of the central principles of efficient or optimal system and growth of capitalism. In reality this principle has not only produced unequal relations so far, but is likely to promote further inequalities so long as trade is between nation-states of unequal sizes, resource endowments, technologies and trade practices. Both Marxists and non-Marxists have turned the division of labour into a normative principle. We often forget that Marx himself had called division of labour the assassination of man. Fourth, an equitable new international economic order requires expanding trade relations because of intensified interdependence through other factors such as technologies, finance and growth. These assumptions are shared by all mainstream economic theories, be they Neo-classical, Keynesian, Marxist, or any other. International Economic Darwinism defies these assumptions.

The theory of International Darwinism stands in sharp contrast to prevailing theories, particularly of interdependence, dependency, the Prebischian theory or of the Brandt Report. Some aspects of Darwinism may be seen reflected in the models of the new international economic order, international division of labour, systems of global classifications, multinationals, spaceship earth, etc., but by and large Darwinism is an alternative explanation or a hypothesis about the position of the South in the global system.

Some analysts have talked about political rather than economic fracturing but as part of certain other problems. For instance, Lukham and Robin say:

> The two dimensions of the crisis, the recession in Capitalism and the *fracturing of the international political order* (emphasis mine) cannot be analysed separately. Yet it is symmetariza-tion of our present condition that they are kept apart. For example, in none of the major negotiations since the early 1970s concerning a New International Economic Order has the control of the global arms race or of the international transfers of weapons figured on the agenda.[1]

It is true that developing nations have a rather small voice in global decision-making but on the surface there is a lot of noise. The UN organizations and the Non-aligned Movement (NAM) which are based on one nation-one vote, appear to give some political clout to developing nations but in essence it comes to very little. It is a cover-up.

There is considerable confusion in the very use of terminology. As mentioned in the Introduction, there are as many classifications as there are schools of thought, international regimes, interests, or ideologies. We intend to focus on contrasting Darwinism with those theories of global ordering which have a strong normative content. To avoid confusion, therefore, we propose to shun the taxonomic approach. Classifications are indiscriminately used even when they do not reflect true reality. Without going into definitional semantics we propose to use two types of classifications:

---

[1] Lukham and Robin, 'Militarization and the New International Arsenals', *Third World Quarterly* (Two), April 1984.

(i) ADCs and LDCs and (ii) North and South. The former classifies nations or nation-states and the latter, the people.

The South comprises the masses who are poor, illiterate, exploited, sub-employed. They are victims of the ADCs as much as of their own ruling elites. There are, however, some exceptions where the ruling elite try to identify their interests with those of the masses, whether successfully or unsuccessfully. By and large the term North includes the rulers in the LDCs or the third world nations. The small percentage who are victimized in the ADCs are even more alienated from their counterparts in the LDCs and hence have no role in the ordering or reordering of the global systems as seen from the South. They should be on the side of the South, but generally are not. Peace movements, the Greens, and human rights groups play a significant role in creating public awareness, but get easily coopted by the North. The Gorbachev-Bush detente has nearly caused their collapse.

II

The term International Economic Darwinism (IED) is defined to include the following set of relations or problems.

First, IED is a set of relations between nations and peoples on the principle of the survival of the fittest, except that nations or peoples do not disappear, if only because it is neither in the interests of the fittest nor in their power to make the unfit completely disappear. They are obliged to make the least fit survive, but only marginally or as destitutes living in ghettos. A few millions may die of starvation, but demography takes care of the numbers. History is replete with cases of genocide or complete wiping out of indigenous populations by colonial marauders. History has also witnessed regrouping of territories and peoples which made new nations out of old ones. And so on. But all that belongs to the past. Modern Darwinism assumes that peoples and nations will generally remain intact. The North-South distinction is derived from this Darwinism, showing that under all assumptions made so far, no matter how the present order is reordered, it will allow the weaker and more unfit to survive but not to participate in and certainly not to decide about the global order. Deviating from his own dependency theory Andre Gunder writes:[2]

[2] Gunder A. Frank, 'World Economic Crisis and Policy Perspective in the Mid 1980s', in *Economic Theory and New World Order*, ed. H.W. Singh etc., Ashish Publishing House, New Delhi, 1987 p. 511.

There has been a radical shift in the international division of labour, in which some lose out in a sort of world game of musical chair. Particularly the leaders lose out and others come to occupy their respective positions and much of the battle is about sharing out the costs and benefits of this major process of re-adjustment in the world economy.

We submit that it is largely beyond the capacity of policy makers to either affect or stem the tide. The dependency theorists never had a solution to the problem they analysed. Now they are accepting their helplessness without realizing that the very analysis they offered was incapable of producing a solution.

Darwinism or rupture theory implies that the ADCs as a group are becoming more and more mutually integrated and thus autonomous of the LDCs. Apparently, the latter's dependence on the former seems to have increased, but in reality the LDCs are being pushed out of the global system to stand on the margin. There is no real periphery in the sense suggested by dependency theorists.

H.W. Singer has defined intra-ADC relations as convergence against the double divergence faced by the LDCs, i.e., divergence from the ADCs as well as internal divergence. This is the central argument of Darwinism or rupture theory. As Singer has stressed, in the LDCs: 'The growth was also divergent in the internal sense, because contrary to what happened elsewhere it was accompanied by increased inequalities in income distribution. Thus both because of divergence between and within countries, Third World poverty did not show any signs of disappearing or even diminishing'.[3] This divergence is one example or principle of Darwinism.

In contrast to interdependence, Darwinism exposes rupture rather than accept integration between North and South in the area of trade which has concealed the rupture for too long. Apparently, the rapid growth in global trade, some net transfer of finance and technology, and the opening up of vast channels of knowledge have created a strong impression of global integration and interdependence. In reality, there is a growing rupture, in respect of economic relations, between ADCs and LDCs as well as between North and South. Darwinism is marked by a declining share of the LDCs in global trade, reverse transfer of resources from the South, a widening technological gap, and unremitting poverty of vast

---

[3] H.W. Singer and others (ed.), *Economic Theory and New World Order*, 1987, pp. 4–5.

masses of the South.[4]

Poverty is now degenerating into both international and national destitution of large sections of the people of the South, into an irreversible process of creating international ghettos. Whatever the claims made on behalf of the ADCs in the system, the number of absolute poor and, more shockingly, the number of absolute destitutes is increasing year by year. There is no hope for them of any kind within the prevailing or suggested models. They form part of international ghettos whose inhabitants are given some crumbs of aid, but without reducing the size of the ghettos. The theory of the reserve army of labour is inapplicable because the ghetto population is unemployable. Darwinism is a theory of slow attrition of millions; it does imply some poverty alleviation but no poverty eradication. The rupturing of economies rests on an international ghetto order.

Rupture is not only between ADCs and LDCs but also within the latter. Indeed most LDCs have been drifting away from one another more sharply than from some of the ADCs. The so-called South-South dialogue has turned out to be a damp squib even though it was admitted that without such a dialogue producing definite results no North-South dialogue was feasible. The way the OPEC nations have exploited other LDCs either directly or in partnership with the ADCs is the most striking example of internal Darwinism among the LDCs. 'At the same time the post-colonial international system has helped to create a harmony of interests between the elites of the Third World and those of the industrialized world, and in the process a conflict of interest between rich countries and poor has been partially transferred into a conflict between the masses and the elites within the poor countries.'[5]

Most theories of exploitation rest on integration between the exploiter and the exploited. The greater the economic exploitation, the greater is the integration between the exploited and the exploiter. One cannot survive without the other. Darwinism goes beyond exploitation. It is a theory of rejection while not ignoring exploitation. Marx's theory of surplus value when applied to international economic relations is sustainable only on the principle of integration. What we see is 'de-integration'. However, Darwinism does suggest the possibility of greater cultural exploita-

[4] Appendix, Tables I and II.
[5] K. Greffin, *International Inequalities and National Poverty*, Macmillan, London, 1978, p. 2.

tion in order to legitimize economic rupture.[6]

International Economic Darwinism is distinct from original Darwinism in that it is more cruel. For a few decades the ADCs showed deep concern about increases in population. Now they have given up. Except for China no other LDC nation is seriously attempting to control population as indeed is reflected in their decennial growth rate. Other statistics do not matter. Earlier, people used to die on account of famines. Now they are preserved at half-starvation levels. They can neither decently survive nor die. All this is a part of the ghetto syndrome. But there is more to it. Nations which contain within their societies large chunks of half-starving people provide the necessary conditions for their marginalization and are subjected to the demand, explicit or implict, of final solution through war or civil strife. Recently well-known ADC economists have called for defining a Fourth World, consisting of sub-Saharan Africa and South Asia. This statement has shocked some Indians but they are refusing to account for their own half-starved, acutely malnutrited, destitute and the marginalized people. Thus for the LDCs, the South, the poor and the destitutes of the world, the most serious crisis is of the onslaught of International Economic Darwinism.

It is necessary to have a clear idea of trade, technology and other economic relations on which our theory is based. The tables in the Appendix give a statistical picture of global trade, manufactures, technology, etc. Table I makes it clear that the share of the third world nations, excluding OPEC and the Gang of Four, has remained around 10 per cent of the total. In recent years, when trade has been expanding, this share has started declining. Between 1980 and 1985 it has declined from 10.5 per cent to 9 per cent. There is nothing to show that it will not decline further. It is equally clear that trade expands fastest within economic blocs. Intra-Comecon and Intra-EEC trade has been increasing the fastest, while trade among the developing countries has not only remained low, but its share is also declining. The so-called South-South trade and cooperation amounts to no more than a propaganda stunt.

The configuration of trade relations, thus, is analogous to the

---

[6] Darwinism dismisses prevailing theories of exploitation. One has to bring in the Gandhian theory of exploitation in which cultural or value exploitation through culture integration is the core of relations between ADCs and LDCs. Economic Darwinism philosophy of cultural universalism.

case in trade theory of a small economy in whose small enough trade the big trading partner has a large share, whereas the former takes a smaller share of the latter. This creates conditions of inequality, dependence, domination and blackmail.

Whosoever else may gain from it, the majority of the LDCs will face drastic reduction in their exports without reduction in imports. The year 1992, when Western Europe will dismantle all trade barriers so that the EEC becomes one big market, will be a disaster year or the beginning of a disastrous phase for the LDCs, particularly for those who now enjoy special benefits.

Table II gives the global picture of technology and direct financial and investment flows of the developing countries and reinforces the inferences drawn from Table I. These figures, taken from UNCTAD and UN Reports, show that direct investment to the developing countries reached its peak in 1981 and declined sharply afterwards. Capital goods exports too declined sharply from that year. Technical assistance, which has been rather small, has remained stagnant.

Tables III and IV point towards a structure of industrial Darwinism. With greater emphasis on import substitution as against export promotion, we may expect a declining share in global trade but compensated significantly by an increasing share in global manufactures. That too has not happened, supporting the theory that the international economic order will remain pitted against the LDCs so long as their policy options are constrained by this order. Darwinism is a true explanation of this order.[7]

Darwinism reminds us of the so-called final solution propounded by Hitler. Now it seems that Hitler was not the last to suggest a final solution. The modern international economic system seems to provide full support to it under cover of interdependence and sweet reasonableness. Darwinism may be too strong a word but responsible economists have used other words to convey the same meaning. The word *Triage*, for instance, has entered into common usage. 'In the pregnant controversies on whether the developed countries have a moral responsibility to share the resources with the third world, are options sometimes advocated, though under a different banner, for instance, triage.'[8] This word was first used with reference to the wounded soldiers during World War I.

---

[7] See also Section VI, below.
[8] James Mittelman, *Out From Development*, Macmillan, London, 1988, pp. 164–65.

Because of scarce medical resources, those who could not be easily saved were deliberately allowed to die. There are many economists who believe that the chunks of human society which cannot be saved should be given the triage treatment.

Similarly, there is the theory of life-boat ethics propounded by Garett Hardin. According to this theory 'those nations which cannot make it on their own should not be admitted to the life-boat of the rich lest we lose our safety factor and threaten our own as well as our progeny's survival'.[9] The ethics of life-boat means that sharing is impossible. As far as Hardin is concerned there are no solutions for the third world countries.

III

More than inequalities of capital and other resources, natural and man-made, it is the growing technological gap between the ADCs and LDCs that lies at the source of Darwinism and the great world disorder, makes the situation explosive and condemns the poor countries to utter physical or intellectual exhaustion (see Table III).

Several distinct trends are noticeable. Both in the ADCs and the LDCs technological developments have given rise to the power of colossal corporations. And it is these corporations with their technological, financial and communication power which have become both the makers of the goods and the makers of the desire for them. Although the high degree of specialization, complexity of decision-making, risk and financial backing that make technological development take the organisational form of big corporations, beyond a certain limit, these corporations break through national barriers to become multinationals.

The present vehicle of this economic domination by the North or the South or more so of the state of Darwinism is the multinational corporation. Over 4,000 of these exist today, most with headquarters in the USA, Europe and Japan. These corporations pick up junior partners from the LDCs, squeeze out small competing firms, evade local taxes through numerous devices, send large profits back to ADCs, and utilise the capital intensive technology that was once used in the industrialized countries successfully dumping them on the LDCs.

Analysts of multinationals (MNCs), be they dependency or interdependence theorists, accept the fact that 'The power of the

---

[9] Garrett Hardin, 'Life Boat Ethics', *Psychology Theory*, Sept. 1984.

global cooperation derives from its unique capacity to use finance, technology and advanced marketing skills to integrate production on a worldwide scale and thus to realize the ancient capitalist dream of one Great Market'.[10] However, one of the important features of these companies is their 'overwhelmingly oligopolistic character, that is, they dominate in markets effectively controlled by a few buyers or sellers'.[11] Their large size, control of technological and product innovation and differentiation, brands and patents, power over investment location, research programme, transfer prices, etc. give multinationals the political power to determine the range of oligopolistic global strategy and a common global control.

Initially in search of markets and profits, the MNCs drove into LDCs with investments, but later their main interests pushed them towards areas which were trade oriented. The ADCs constituted the areas dominated by trade. The LDCs both welcomed them as well as repelled them, depending upon their own evaluation. Those who welcomed them without safeguards came to grief because of the economic control exercised by the MNCs. Those who tried to repel them but failed to develop their own science and technology base also came to grief because they lost the trade leverage and ultimately had to reverse their negative attitude.

Multinationals may be in private hands as in the west, semi-public enterprises, again as in the west, or fully owned and controlled by the state, as in the communist countries. Now these multinationals take recourse to and finally work for countries which have reached a certain stage of development. In countries below that level of development, namely the LDCs, the restrictions they impose with respect to technological diffusion of technology, export markets, domestic competition, etc. make the MNCs barriers to growth because they create enclaves and impose a new dualism on an existing dualistic economy inherited from the colonial era.

However, whatever the MNC package, the LDCs were not allowed to determine the appropriateness of commodity production and technological use. The net result was the perpetuation of domestic dualism of the colonial era and this ensured profits for the

[10] R.J. Barnet and R.E. Muller, *Global Reach: The Power of the Multinational Corporations*, op. cit.

[11] D. Colman and F. Nixon, *Economics of Change in Less Developed Countries*, Philip Allan, Oxford, 1978, p. 219.

MNCs. MNCs determine the share of trade for LDCs as prompted by their global strategies as well as by the aforementioned dualism. Since the trend is towards greater trade integration among the ADCs for a variety of reasons discussed earlier, trade in the LDCs loses its autonomous character. Thus the MNCs, with their control over resources, oligopolistic power and focus on economic development of the ADCs, ultimately marginalize and darwinize the LDCs first in trade and then through trade, in the technological development of LDCs, ironically enough, by operating within the LDCs. MNCs thus assume a double role of domination over LDCs.

We know that 75 per cent of the western world's production comes from between 1000 and 2000 firms. In the United States 60 per cent of the national capital is in the hands of just 200 firms. In France, where integration is considerably less advanced, 0.4 per cent of business enterprises, that is to say 800 firms, are responsible for 37 per cent of total production. Similarly international interests are the prerogative of a restricted number of firms: just 165 British firms are responsible for 80 per cent of overseas investments; in Germany 82 firms provide 70 per cent of foreign investments; three-quarters of United States' external investment comes from 190 firms.[12] The general trend is that a few oligopolistic firms control anywhere between one-half to two-thirds of the total production of the world. This control is exercised against the independence of the LDCs.

Another impact of the technological gap is the shift from turning to old colonies as sources of raw materials and markets for the goods of metropolitan powers, to seeing them as new instrument markets for second-rate industrial countries. More significantly, it is the transfer of light industries into areas of cheap labour that marks the new phase. Goods requiring sophisticated technologies are kept at industrial centres and those using limited technologies are spread out.

Professor Meister has drawn attention to this and another allied problem.

> The transfer of light industry to zones of cheap, competent and docile labour—as is the case today in South-East Asia—means a comparable reduction in the number of immigrant workers at home, and hence helps to diminish racial ill-

12 Ibid.

feeling with its unfortunate consequences of industrial and social unrest. Similarly, on the model of tax havens the absence of anti-pollution legislation (or the flouting there-fore) in the poor countries creates real 'havens for pollu-ters'—. So a new style of international division of labour is gradually coming into being, the rich countries keeping the highly capitalized industries with the clean factories to them-selves, while the poor countries manufacture labour-inten-sive products involving dirty factories.[13]

In this milieu, it is becoming increasingly difficult for any single country to find a natural and indigenous solution for its socio-economic problem. This inability leads to serious political compli-cations. It is not surprising that both Washington and Moscow denounce the so-called narrow nationalism of the poor and newly independent countries. The US has started a tirade against impor-tant LDCs such as India, Brazil, etc. These countries are being sucked into this new economic order without their consent, an order which condemns them to live in perpetual poverty. Even the poorest nation is being forced to put all its eggs in the export basket. This is the practice today. It was not so ten or fifteen years ago even, when the economic plight of these countries was unenviable.

Modern technological regimes are formed not by nations but by economic organizations and interests on the one hand and by scientists and technological experts on the other. Every powerful nation tries to keep control over both because in the final analysis they find that their competitiveness and productivity increases depend upon their control of technologies. It is the economic nationalism of the ADCs which is most fiercely reflected in their national technological regimes. Even within the alliance system, secretiveness, jealousies and desire for appropriation in respect of technologies remain a critical barrier for further integration. Unlike the international trading regimes such as GATT and other organi-zations, there are no comparable international technological re-gimes. They are secretive arrangements. The day such regimes come into being, the monopoly of a few powerful nations over the rest would be complete, and the global order would be fractured in every sense of the word. Before such a calamity comes upon us it is important that a more equitable and ecologically justifiable world

[13] Ibid., quoted.

of technological progress be created.

Notwithstanding all the promises that the MNCs and technological regimes make they are unwilling to alleviate the position of
the vast starving millions as well as of less illiterate and semi-
educated masses, whose health is jeopardized not only by the rest
of the socio-economic regimes but also by the technological regimes. It is obvious that as technological progress continues, new
disparities and exploitations are also created. Those who are focusing entirely on the elimination of nuclear weapons seem to have
ignored the fact that it is not weapons but restricted technological
regimes which threaten humanity.

The prevailing technological and scientific regimes are dominated by the production of weapon systems on the one hand and
technologies which either focus on consumer durables or on information, on the other. Of course, there are new frontiers of space,
bio-technology and genetics about which the world is still hopeful.
However, it seems that the global economic system, knowledge
order and security system have become components of and are
being dominated by new technologies created in the wake of
technological regimes.

Several approaches to technological development have been
suggested by the LDCs in an attempt to follow the examples of the
ADCs. The four most important are: (i) the 'catch-up' technology
approach, (ii) 'technology-following' strategies, (iii) technology
adoption and diffusion, and (iv) science and knowledge self-reliant
approach. Many LDCs have opted for one or more of these approaches. The question is: why have some failed, and others succeeded? The answer can be found in the overall approach of the
development strategies. Those nations which imported technologies in the short run but developed them later with their own R&D
base, introduced stiff domestic competition, made investment in
high productivity areas, whether for domestic use or export, dis-
criminated between domestic and foreign entrepreneurs, etc.,
succeeded. On the other hand, those which did not follow this
policy, failed. All the success stories can be summed up as a
'Swadeshi' approach or self-reliance approach. If a developing
country can develop technological capacities very early in production without assimilation of foreign technology, it can become self-
reliant. The important issue is the avoidance of foreign control over
technology.

Most of the LDCs cannot be on the frontiers of technology, but they can certainly imitate, adapt and develop their own R&D or bypass ADCs' technologies to fight back the onslaught of the products of ADCs. The central problem is that even with relatively low levels of knowledge and early stages of industrialization, a developing country can avoid dumping of second-rate industries by the ADCs. As Westphal, Rhee and Pursell (1981) have stated:

> South Korea's technological mastery has progressed much further in plant operation than in plant and product design. It thus appears that the know-how to operate production processes efficiently is to a large degree, independent of the ability to use the underlying engineering principles in investment activity. . . . That is not to deny that . . . Koreans have become increasingly involved in various phases of project implementation, it is not too great an overstatement to say that Korea has become a significant industrial power simply on the basis of efficiency in production.[14]

The LDCs now face new problems with the extraordinary growth in technologies and knowledge. In the last few decades, there has been a qualitative change. An increasing number of technologies have become science-based, a situation strikingly different from that of the nineteenth century. Accordingly, without high-level domestic science capability, imitation and adaptation have become difficult. As suggested by Freeman, Clark and Soete (1982): 'It may become increasingly difficult to borrow or imitate without a reasonably high-level domestic science capability. . . . If this turns out to be so, it may be important in slowing down the progression of the less-industrial   countries to increasingly complex, research-intensive production.'[15] These capacities are also controlled by the MNCs.

Probably, the most important aspect of the situation today is that the technological developments in the ADCs have very little to do with the needs of those in the LDCs. As Kaplinsky (1984c) puts it:

[14] L.E. Westphal, Y.W. Rhee, and G. Pursell, 1981, 'Korean Industrial Competence: Where it Came From', Washington, DC: World Bank, Staff Working Paper No. 469.

[15] C. Freeman, J. Clark and L. Soete, *Unemployment and Technical Innovation: A Study of Long Waves and Economic Development*, London, 1982, Frances Pinter.

The assertion that LDCs can continue to assimilate DC technology at an unchanged rate, that they can continue their
penetration of DC markets in increasingly technology-intensive manufactures, must be opened to question. In contrast, I
offer a view that suggests that the gap between DC and LDC
technology is reopening, but at the same time DC technology
is becoming increasingly inappropriate for LDCs.[16]

Consequently, a rigid dependency or rupture has become the
distinct characteristic of relations between the ADCs and LDCs.
Technological Darwinism has become the central core of global
Darwinism.

One reason is that life-cycle of many products suggests that as
high-technology products mature and stabilise, new possibilities
emerge that make their production more compatible with the
relative factor prices when skills and resources available in less-
advanced economies are married to them. Sometime incremental
rather than basic designing skills play the central role and even
these are denied to the LDCs. There seems to be many opportunities
for modifications in final product design or specification that will
make high-technology products far more compatible with the
capabilities of less-advanced economies.

Today the general discussion between 'generation' and 'diffusion' of technology has become inappropriate, since technologies
are modified, adjusted and improved upon in the process of their
diffusion. It must be recognised that cumulative significance of
incremental improvements requires that the processes of diffusion
and technological change need to be conceptually linked. It may
well be taken that part of the reason for Japan's successful 'catch up'
and, in some cases, 'take over' lies in the technical change generated
by rapid but autonomous diffusion which was itself facilitated by
appropriate socio-political relations and fuelled by high rates investment. Foreign collaborators with MNCs specifically put restriction on any kind of diffusion.

There is a danger of the so-called 'catch up' strategy for several
reasons. The catch for the catch-up approach is also with the MNCs.
Other resources are: (a) there can be no catching up between most

[16] R. Kaplinsky, 'Trade in Technology—Who, What, Where and When?', in
Fransman and King (1984).

R. Kaplinsky, forthcoming, 'Microelectronics and the Onset of Systemofacture:
Some Implications for Third World Industrialisation', World Development.

advanced and most undeveloped countries because of knowledge explosion and rapid increases in technology and knowledge; (b) circumstances differ so much from industry to industry that no general technology policy can be meaningful; (c) improvements can only be of incremental nature in the use of domestic or imported technologies; (d) science-based knowledge may become difficult in the short run; (e) the quality of product of foreign manufacturers may be distinctively better and unbeatable in competition; (f) major problem in 'catch up' strategy is in the initial selection by private firms or by the states; the decision may be influenced by trade circumstances; (g) conflict between short-run and long-run criteria; (h) sequence in developing deeper levels of knowledge in the industries that have been selected require a variety of policies all of which may not be available. In the early stages of industrialisation, the possibility of 'catch up' process requires relatively low level of knowledge. It is not true today, as the production skills today require more complicated aappied research as well as basic research. The sequence has changed because deeper knowledge is required in order to facilitate routine production.

As against the 'catching up' strategy, there is the 'technology following' strategy. It is here that MNCs exercise their full control. Indeed both strategies widen the technological gap because of the absence of clear self-reliant science and technology plans. The latter differs from former in the sense that it relies on the use of foreign knowledge efficiently without in the long-run building up the capabilities to challenge the frontier leaders. The strategy does not preclude the selection of infant industries, but the hope that these industries will become internationally efficient with the passage of time is no longer valid. Investment and knowledge-creating capabilities have to be adequately developed with the utilization of foreign knowledge productively.

Once a country refuses to accept the mere 'catch up' or 'follow up' technology approach, it can break the international technology leadership. That is why the history has shown that international technology leadership is difficult to sustain. In recent years, the Japanese firms, first by imitation and then by development of R&D have overtaken most of the developed nations. They understood and mastered international technology diffusion process. As W.A. Lewis (1957) stated: 'It is not necessary to be a pioneer in order to have large export trade. It is sufficient to be a quick imitator. Britain would have done well enough if she merely imitated German and

American innovations. Japan, Belgium and Switzerland owe more of their success as exporters of manufacturers to imitation than they do to innovation.'[17]

The choice will have to be made between import of foreign knowledge and foreign technology in various forms and use of both market and non-market processes such as direct foreign investment, licensing and other know-how agreements, imitation, scanning of foreign trade journals and learning-by-exporting. 'Technology following' becomes very difficult with the process of knowledge and financing as required by industries. The real problem is one of 'keeping-up' rather than of 'catching-up'.

The prospects are not too bright for both. The LDCs, particularly India, in their trying to enter into software market so as to emerge as a major offshore centre for software production, face a wall. According to a recent International Labour Organization (ILO) study, the prospects for these low-wage, manpower-rich nations in tapping the employment and income potential of the burgeoning software industry were not too bright. This was not because of any lack in technical expertise, but because of a host of other bottlenecks such as the absence in many third world countries of infrastructurtal and other facilities, the study said.

The world market for software and computing services, which doubled in the first half of the 1980s to about $ 55 billion, is forecast to rise to $ 163 billion by 1991 and to about $ 340 billion by 1996. It said the demand for packaged software would continue to grow rapidly, while the demand for data processing would decline.

Though it looked as if trade in software and computer services would continue to remain in the private preserve of the more advanced countries, the study said in many developing countries, technological capability was existent but not exploited. One reason is brain drain.

Incidentally, a survey carried out in 1985 in the US showed that foreign and naturalized citizens constituted 30 per cent of the scientists and engineers in the computer and electronic industries—a proportion much higher than the average for all industries.[18]

To think of self-reliant technological change in the short-run, for producing internationally efficient products is not the correct

[17] W.A. Lewis. 'International Competition in Manufactures', *American Economic Review Papers and Proceedings*, Vol. 47, May 1957.

[18] The Economic Times,New Delhi, dt. 2 August, 1990.

approach. One has to think of the long-term cost-benefits, particularly those of the transformation of domestic resources directly into locally-generated technologies. In fact, import of technology and generating domestic technologies are not mutually exclusive. It is technological and not a generalized economic self-reliance that is the answer to Darwinism.

IV

Few will disagree with the proposition that South Asia is very unstable, economically backward, politically prone to violence and most susceptible to interference from outside powers. Indo-Pakistan relations have had a chequered history of wars, conflicts and rivalries to which Indo-Bangla and Indo-Sri Lanka relations are adding new complications. If Afghanistan is included in the scenario, and there is no reason not to include it, South Asia cannot be expected to show signs of stability in the foreseeable future.

The African countries have woken up only recently to the danger of large parts of Africa becoming a dust bowl as well as dust bin for the dumping of dangerous industrial and nuclear wastes. For nearly 20 years now western companies have been dumping dangerous wastes in Africa because they found it more expensive to do so elsewhere. Small African countries have been lured into accepting wastes because some of them are so poor that the money offered in exchange is more than their national budgets.

The people of the South Asian and African countries are victims of their own government propaganda. The latter have developed vested interests in inter-state conflicts, whether inherited from the colonial past or newly created. The ruling elites of these countries have developed a vested interest in maintaining situations of enmities and rivalries and the capacity to invite foreign powers, in the name of national independence and national security. For decades now the arms race, from which the sellers of arms have benefited, has been carefully planned by the big powers. So much so that today the defence budgets of these countries are crippling their economies.

The global power structure has taken a new turn in its understanding and policy options towards South Asia and parts of Africa, particularly in the field of economics. There is a set of economists who belong to the developed world and influence the nature of economic thrusts of developed nations into the underdeveloped world and they have created a new entity called the fourth world which would consist of South Asia, Sub-Saharan African nations and a few other micro states. This entity is different from the one which was carved out as the third world. The fourth world will not consist of more than twenty countries.

The fourth world is defined in terms of its per capita income but the implications are much more sinister. It is presumed that the fourth world nations have very poor prospects of development, and the restructuring of the rest of the global economic system will have to be done without considering these nations as relevant. Aid would be available but the strategies of development as defined by international agencies would be such as would be suitable for an international ghetto. The current level of per capita income, around 300 dollars, or a little more or less, is not going to change even in the twenty-first century as far as one can foresee.

These countries have landed themselves into many ecological disasters and are continuing anti-ecological policies. There are environmental groups making noises but their impact is negligible. It seems that short-term growth is being planned at the cost of long-term development. Many natural thresholds have been crossed, drastic climatic changes are taking place to wipe out the fruits of past development and, above all, more and more of the poor are turned into destitutes. Economic difficulties are leading to new social conflicts and violence.

A United Nations Population Fund Seminar which was held in May 1988 in London and in which some of the world's best known experts participated came to a rather depressing conclusion for India. The most critical conclusion was:

> India today is poised between China and Africa. The right decisions could propel it rapidly towards China which is showing signs of overcoming its vast development problems. But failure to take the right steps urgently could push India into the famine and despair engulfing sub-Saharan Africa.

The seminar focused on three indicators: (i) food production, (ii) population control, and (iii) control of environmental degradation. India at the moment is delicately and desperately balanced between China and Africa. In other words, it is a choice between economic collapse some time in the future and a permanent solution to both food and population.

At the face of it, the purpose of this recategorization is to demand larger transfer of resources; in reality this exercise is a subtle design to marginalize the so-called fourth world nations, to remove them from global decision-making. Paul Streetan, who has much to do with World Bank strategies, says: 'concern with creating the international system has, at least in rhetoric, been closely linked with concern for the world's poor. But the poor are largely in what is sometimes called the Fourth World: South-Asia, Sub-Saharan Africa and a few Islands.'

In an earlier debate, edited by Jagdish Bhagwati, it was surmised that political and economic issues interact in two very important ways. First, the third world wants more political power partly in order to promote its economic objectives. But the immediate targets of its international efforts differ importantly from the targets of the fourth world. The third world countries concentrate largely on acquiring new economic opportunities: access to the markets of the industrialized countries for export of manufactured goods, access to international capital markets, and access to modern technology. The fourth world, on the other hand, continues to stress its need for resource transfers through the traditional medium of foreign aid.

This important difference between the goals of the third and fourth worlds, however, is reconciled by the second interaction between politics and economics of the debate over a New International Economic Order (NIEO): the importance to the third world of championing the aspirations of the fourth world. This objective is particularly important to the OPEC countries, who wish desperately to avoid political isolation and universal condemnation for disrupting the world economy with their massive increase in the price of oil. To achieve that end and to fight Darwinism, they must retain the support of the other developing countries—no mean task, since those countries have suffered severely from that event.

The main features of the fourth world are as follows. First, the per capita growth in these countries has been between 1 and 1.5 per cent per annum. Since most of this has not gone to the poor, the number of the poor has been swelling. For instance, even by official criteria, which is no longer relevant as it is based on defective and outdated factors, the number of the poor living in India is more than the entire population at the time of independence.

Second, in recent years the ugly fact has come out that the fourth world nations have large sections of the population going through biological decay. As early as the Third Plan, the Indian Planning

Commission had admitted that it could not do anything to uplift the bottom 20 per cent of the population who were destitutes. Later on this mistake was corrected by introducing with great flourish many anti-poverty programmes. Unfortunately, after about 15 years it is clear that the bottom 20 per cent of the population remains un-touched. Consumption in crude calories is below 1000 per day. They have practically no access to clean drinking water, sanitation and public health.

Third, in some of the fourth world nations, near famine condi-tions are re-appearing. Others, like South Asia, which have appar-ently done well in food production, have so mismanaged their environment and so much degraded their land that they either face epidemics of various kinds or so much increase in the cost of access to other requirements, such as fodder, fuel, water and natural vegetation for human consumption, that the total cost of agricul-tural output is turning out to be more than the value of the output.

Fourth, notwithstanding all efforts, the share of trade of the entire fourth world is about one per cent of the total and despite the massive attempts to promote exports this share is threatening to decline further. In fact, during the last two decades the share has been going down slightly.

Fifth, the global strategies for aid and transfer of funds and technologies, to provide investments, etc. for the fourth world seem to be no different, but in reality they are very dissimilar. The main thrust is on municipal government-like policies for slum areas. Even a slum strategy has some meaning because slums provide labour inputs to the city's active population and are thus integrated with others. In the case of the fourth world the attempt is to de-integrate or exclude it from the global system.

Sixth, it seems that the fourth world has crossed many more natural thresholds from which if there is no comeback short-term growth itself will decline. One of the factors that inhibits growth is the high rate of population growth. The whole development strategy adopted now has been exposed to have no impact on the birth rate.

Therefore, it seems that the assumptions of the international global order in respect of the fourth world are based on very rational calculations, suggesting that some nations which are now called the fourth world have fewer long-term prospects. But there is an additional factor, namely, that this area is also politically unstable, infested with inter-state wars and prone to violence. There is little chance of stemming the forces of social decay. The ruling elite can be bought over at a cheap price and they will be obliged to maintain these ghettos. This is the core of Daewinism.

The problem of the style of life and corruption of the ruling elite in the fourth world is creating a new global dimension of disgust about corruption amidst poverty as well as plenty. Three-fourths of the aid goes to public sector plants from which the political and bureaucratic elite profit both legally and illegally. There is something secretive about aid and assistance. According to the international financial institutions India's external financial obligations are somewhere around 60 to 70 billion dollars. At the current rate of borrowing and foreign aid, including normal escalation, India's foreign debt would be about 125 billion dollars by the mid-1990s. But the important differences between India and Brazil would be that India's per capita income will remain about one-fifth of Brazil's. The position of other so-called fourth world nations is worse. The lower interest burden is due to past concessional aid. Claim to concessional aid is not likely to square up with claims and boasts of rapid industrialization, technological development and food self-sufficiency. The concessional aid is tied to the base of graduation towards development. India's claim that it has used aid well is one argument. However, what matters is on what terms it gets more aid and the same applies to the other fourth world countries. In about a little more than a decade the fourth world would go externally bankrupt, particularly because its share in global trade is unlikely to improve even marginally. With one-fifth of Brazil's per capita income but external debt reaching the level of Brazil, India will be a basket case of a debt trap.

It seems strange that South-Asia, particularly India, should be equated with Sub-Saharan Africa. India's two achievements, one in respect of food production and the other in respect of high rate savings, are enough to reject her being included in this category. It is the long term which seems to point to the other direction. Environment experts accept that India's food production will go down in the beginning of the twenty-first century, while its population will continue to increase.

Paradoxically, India is being accepted as a new regional military power which may entitle her some role assigned by the great powers. Henry Kissinger has openly suggested that India should take over some of the responsibilities of the US in this region. The statement came as a pleasant surprise to Indians who have been demanding precisely such a role or certification from the west. Implicitly, the Soviet Union had accepted that role for India in 1971 and maintained her foreign policy objectives. However, the burden of the defence expenditure weighs heavily on fiscal balance.

Notwithstanding all the noises made by the big powers about India and Pakistan developing nuclear weapons, there is little serious concern. The west, particularly the US, has helped Pakistan in her programme and India had been preparing her own programmes without much fuss. All that the big powers are doing is to calculate how many millions will die in the event of a India-Pakistan nuclear confrontation. How can the nuclear race during the two countries be stopped if large-scale sale of arms to them continues and heavy military expenditure is incurred.

Therefore, the new category of the fourth world means the creation of Darwinism's international ghetto which can be left to its own device for survival or destruction. Some aid would be available on a declining basis, weapons would be sold or given free and the nations so defined would be kept out of global power systems. The would-be untouchables of the world have been christened the fourth world.

THEORY OF DEPENDENCY

The central theme of this essay is to provide a critique of the two dramatically opposed theories of global order from the standpoint of Darwinism and then reflect back upon the latter from the viewpoints of those theories, namely, interdependence and dependency. Other alternatives are taken care of as they are some combination of the two.

Let us state here the definitional distinction between Darwinism and dependency theory, with which it seems to have a large resemblance, and between Darwinism and interdependence, to which it is totally contrary. Though the most critical assumption of dependency is the same as of interdependence, the crucial difference is that the former is assumed as a zero sum game and the latter as a positive sum game. An even stronger assumption is that these are two sides of the same game. In terms of game theoretics, Darwinism is a negative sum game in which one side is not allowed to play except as a dummy resulting from the same game, though it bears the brunt of the negative impact of the relationship.

Dependency theory is quite well known and therefore needs no elaboration. But, since it is to be contrasted with Darwinism, its critique is a part of this book. For its statements, however, no more than a summary is given.

Although the dependency theory 'was never a theory in the true sense of the word', it has all the necessary parameters of a theory except that it could neither predict nor prescribe. It has a powerful explanatory force which is universally recognized. Basically, it is a theory of exploitation based on class conflict, unevenness of development, national differences and conflicts of interests. Its main inspiration comes from the Marxist-Leninist theories but it has developed its own special paradigm.

Although there is no single dependency theory, all theorists share a common perspective which establishes a relation between what is called the core or centre and the periphery within an international system. In other words, dependency is a theory which relates to an international system based on specific relations between the two as well as within each. However, within the dependency system, a certain degree of interdependence is recognized, particularly in respect of domestic social change or war or revolution as an autonomous force and the international system. There are also certain ambivalent situations that the theory cannot meet. Nevertheless, dependency has a strong hypothesis and a large part of the world seems to conform to it. If the theory is somewhat blurred, it is because its theorists have not taken care of what the theory normatively requires.

A generalized dependency theory is as follows: Capitalism must accumulate and expand to survive and consequently it must expand into other territories in search of higher profits. Through investments in developing or colonial or semi-colonial countries, more resources are transferred back to the advanced countries both overtly and covertly. Consequently the weaker nation is 'decapitalized' and its development constrained. Another way of exploitation is through the manipulation of trade and exchange rates, particularly the creation of unequal exchange relations. It is a part of the general theory that a permanent deterioration in terms of trade takes place. In other words, exploitation is both direct and indirect and the more the developing countries try to push forward through this interaction the more quickly they get trapped in dependency. Ultimately, positive transfer of resources turns into negative transfer. Multinationals and their subsidiaries further stunt growth. Imports and exports are overinvoiced and underinvoiced, respectively, and thus illegal transfer takes place in which the local trader acts as a junior partner. The crisis of development or underdevelopment in developing countries becomes sharp when the developed countries go through normal trade cycles. Once this situation gets established through 'unequal exchange', a developing country slips into or is pushed into a new phase of 'structural dependency'. All this implies that dependence on the ADCs gets firmly rooted in the economic, social, political and military structure of the LDCs as a result of foreign domination that originated in the colonial form. The new ruling classes of the LDCs become partners in this exploitation by their neglect of an indigenous capital goods base and autonomous technologies. Domestic resources are concentrated on the modern enclave sector whose goods are for consumption of the elite and middle classes or for export. Dependence is fully internalized by which external relations get quickly absorbed in the domestic economy whereas rural labour, the more abundant factor, is pushed into the traditional static sector.

The theory emanates from a rather crucial premise, namely the failure of the bourgeoisie to perform its historic role of development of domestic capitalism and creation of an autonomous industrial system. The same applies to the role of the other class, namely the industrial proletariat, because of its quantitative insufficiency, its embourgeoisement or its internal divisions. Some argue that if one recognizes this basic premise, then the peasantry as a class has to be assigned a role which is denied to classical classes for revolution or any other transformation. The dependency theory is very weak in dealing with the peasantry.

The most important version of the dependency theory is derived from the Leninist theory of imperialism. Karl Marx himself never formulated any such theory but the dependency theorists call themselves Marxists though each has a different version. For instance, Cardose and Fletto declare that 'a system is dependent when the accumulation and expansion of capital cannot find its essential dynamic component inside the system'. This could be straight from Lenin but there are other versions.

Mandel has tried to identify three Marxist scenarios of modern imperialism, all of which can be encased within dependency: (i) supraimperialism, i.e., dominance of a single imperial power; (ii) ultraimperialism, i.e., internationalization of capital over the state or states; and (iii) interimperialism, i.e., the creation of a small number of imperialist 'superpowers' which are prevented from becoming superimperialism because of the uneven development of capital.[1] These are simple rationalizations of a difficult situation in order to put it into a single Marxist mould. No serious differences in approaches, policies or conclusions arise no matter what scenario is accepted. The socalled uneven development of capital is a ghost which Marxists have always cherished without giving it a historical meaning and ignoring that uneven development is very

[1] Ernest Mandel, *Late Capitalism*, 1975, p. 332.

much present within all socialist societies. Yet unevenness is a fact on which dependency heavily relies. Unfortunately, for the dependency theorists never has there been a situation of evenness anywhere.

The third world debt, which is an expression of both imperialism and internal colonialism, has reached the figure of nearly 1300 billion dollars. Three-fourths of this debt is medium and long term. Three-fourths of this is private, the rest is owned by governments of the developed world. Of the short-term debt, about 20 per cent is owed to IMF. Debt amortization and interest payments amount to about 13 per cent of the total. The ratio of debt services to export now varies between 25 to 130 per cent. What is most interesting is that the transfer of profits is only 15 billion dollars. This figure is so small that it nearly knocks off the Leninist theory altogether. The most rapacious side of imperialism which cannot be explained by any past theory is that after four decades of aid nearly 30 billion dollars form net reverse transfers from the developing to the developed world. The most interesting aspect of the present-day debt burden is that it is threatening to knock off a lot of economic relations between ADCs and LDCs if debt is not slashed.

Dependency theorists have held the view that the epicentre of the global economic crisis is and has been the heart of the capitalist system, the position of the heart changing from one set of nations to another and from one historical period to another. The empirical proof in support was presented in the form of rather too neatly arranged cycles of growth. The cycles were of three types: long cycles of Kondritieff ranging from 40 to 50 years; intermediate cycles of Juglar having a life of about 10 years, and finally the short cycles. During the last 200 years, the trade cycle analysts tell us, there were eight Kondritieff waves, 20 Juglar intermediate cycles and some 60 odd short cycles. Each new cycle is a new circus of imperialism. Whatever the cycle, of course, the peripheries have suffered. However, what has been missed by dependency theorists is that these cycles led to 'shattering individual economies and setting one economy against another as each nation has tried to protect itself against destructive economic forces'.[2]

If Marx unfolded for us the rise of the Age of Capital and hoped that it will be replaced by the Age of Labour, i.e., a new international division of labour, he has yet to be proved right. The Age of Capital

---

[2] Robert Gilpin, *The Political Economy of International Relations*, Princeton, 1987, p. 105.

has been replaced by the Age of Technology, almost completely bypassing the Age of Labour. In the socialist countries, capital accumulation was achieved with vengence and this was done not only by eliminating the political power of labour but by positively repressing and insulting labour.

The global system of trade and exchange can no longer conceal the tragedy of domination of both man and nature by economic and political systems and by a power elite lending to the depletion of both spiritual values and natural resources. Corporate interests and state sectors are predatory forces preying upon both man and nature. The result is brilliantly analysed by Stephen G. Bunker: 'each human intervention in the environment transforms it in ways which limit the possibilities of subsequent interventions'. This is one major cost of trade and development which is not covered by any cost analysis. History has moved in a certain direction to produce disasters. A bigger disaster is that it is moving even now, faster than before, in the same direction. An analysis of the 'relations between world systems of exchange and the social, evolutionary series of ecosystemic transformation from the time of colonial contact until the present' shows that the same relationships are more ruthlessly pursued. No wonder Bunker comes to the conclusion that the only way to stop this process is for the local systems in the peripheral regimes that are being exploited to develop self-sustaining symbiosis and economics which can preserve the ecosystems.[3] This would be possible only if the local groups and areas are not allowed to be preyed upon by trading predators.

In the advanced capitalist countries in which Social Democratic and Labour parties came to power, the model produced was of a corporate system in which labour was accepted in a junior position with capital. The two together exploited the LDCs and made the ruling elites of the latter, including the educational elites, as partners. The ungovernability of the LDCs was the result of this exploitation as well as the greed of the ruling elites of the LDCs, or of both.

The critique of the dependency theory has been more elaborate than the statement of the theory because of its oversimplification. The dependency theorists have not succeeded in answering the objections which are quite a few. These objections will be simply enumerated as background and not discussed in detail.

First, the theory gives much less weight to domestic factors and

[3] Stephen Bunker, *Understanding the Amazon*, University of Illinois, 1985.

specific historical conditions, political processes, institutions, and cultural factors which affect the economic policies and strategies of a nation. Indeed it makes no distinction between one dependent state and another. The asymmetry of international relations is seen in the extreme as producing invariant relations. The theory ignores the forces of nationalism as much as the case of those countries which have been able to develop at least some kind of semi-autonomous system.

Second, the theory rests on a one-sided relationship. It accepts the primacy of economics over everything else. In fact, without this economic determinism, the theory will collapse. But this economism is derived from Marxism in its Leninist version. For instance, the situation of several Latin American nations in which the military has assumed an autonomous political role cannot be explained entirely in terms of economic relations. The domestic economic political and social structure, for instance of Chile, always was and still remains determined first and foremost by the fact and specific nature of its participation in the old capitalist system.

In this characterization of the dependent economy, the Marxists and non-Marxists have also combined their respective concepts to confuse the picture. The non-Marxists, like Prebisch, use alternative concepts of income groups in place of classes, or macro-level relations in place of international surplus value. The two are sometimes called extremists and moderates respectively but basically both contribute to the dependency theory, one coming from economism and the other exclusively taking an impersonal approach. This can be described as 'double determinism' in dependency writing.

Third, no matter how the international economic relations are organized, so long as nations are unequal in size, resources and technologies, there would always be asymmetry in these relations. The tendency of the strong to exploit the weak will not disappear under any system. It will disappear only with a world government or by the boycott of big nations by small nations. The problems created by the inequality of nations is as clearly highlighted within the communist system of Eastern Europe as in the capitalist countries.

Fourth, although some of the dependency theorists have recognized the internal problems of the core countries, they have not been able to explain why and how the relations within the core can also assume a dependency character. For instance, Canada and

Belgium are dominated by foreign multinationals as are many other developing countries. Generally, the multinationals treat both the developed and the developing countries as one common market and pursue more or less the same strategies and use the same technologies. Therefore, if pushed to the limit, the dependency theory would suggest that there are only two or three nations and several multinationals which are independent, and the rest of the world is dependent. This approach will put many poor and rich nations in one group, ruling out policy options for the LDCs.

Fifth, there are two other versions of dependency, namely, dependency as a relation between systems, and dependency as a conditioning factor which alters internal functions, policies and institutions by a dependent social formation. This distinction is made for convenience rather than for any rigorous analysis although the distinction, if proved to be correct, can be very useful. The analogy of backward regions within nations being dependent upon and having development conditioned by the power of the developed regions is brought to mind. The dependency theory either ignores this distinction or offers opposing views.

Sixth, a large number of countries have been able to come out of a pure dependency situation through industrialization, agricultural development and even technological improvement. The development of some East Asian countries, which has pushed them into the first world, reveals not only a high degree of industrialization but social development in the field of education and health that can be comfortably compared with the developed countries. On the other hand, countries like Canada, Australia and New Zealand which fall between the core and the periphery are struggling against big brothers.

Seventh, the theory rests on a stagnationist view of economies and economic relations. This is empirically incorrect within the frame of the theory itself. For instance, industrialization can lead to greater dependency or autonomy depending upon the nature of programmes of industrialization. The dependency theory assumes only a one-sided relationship.

Eighth, the pessimism of the dependency theory is very deep indeed. The case for a socialist revolution is built on the early or ultimate disappearance of the national bourgeoisie. Not only did the third world national bourgeoisie not disappear, it was very much active in building relations with both the western and eastern developed nations. This pessimism arises from suggesting the im-

possible. When nations do not have even elementary class formations and the society and economy are dominated more by non-
class than class forces, who is to bell the cat of revolution? Implicitly
and explicitly, dependency theorists exhort people to move to
urban terrorism in the name of revolution.

Dos Santos, a dependency theorist, tried to save the theory from
its dogmatism by bringing back the national bourgeoisie into the
theory as against its assumed disappearance. He argued that the
national bourgeoisie was assimilated and not eliminated by the
international bourgeoisie. The bourgeoisie played the role of
'dominated dominers' who also dominated the domestic economy.
But, like Gunder Frank, Dos Santos fell prey to empiricism. The
absence of rapid growth of capital goods was interpreted as the
dominant characteristic of the periphery. The capital goods industry could not develop despite the clamour from all sides for the
transfer of capital and technology for assisting developing countries and having a new international economic order. In reality
these transfers and not their absence lay at the root of dependency
and stunted growth. Even China learnt the bitter lesson that Soviet
transfer of technology was a road to dependency.

Samar Amin has dealt with the same issue in terms of unequal
exchange. There are a dozen reasons why unequal exchange occurs
in trade between the centre and the periphery. Trade must produce
unequal exchange among unequals. But Amin concentrated on a
rather weak aspect, namely, low wage export because of the absence of an adequate domestic market. The imports, on the other
hand, being capital intensive and based on a high wage structure,
were relatively over-priced. Prebisch had given this and other
reasons in a more sophisticated way but there is ample evidence to
show that wage determination in the developing nations remains
the least important aspect of unequal exchange relations.

Ninth, dependency theory takes its origin from colonial hypothesis. Imperialism was a domination that depended on economic relations. However, there are nations which have never been
under any colonial power and yet are no better than former colonies. Thailand, Ethiopia and Liberia did not suffer under prolonged
colonial domination.

Tenth, probably the most stringent criticism of the dependency
theory has come from its cavalier attitude to definition and empirical evidence. A strong hypothesis and a high level of abstraction
will at least require a very precise definition on the basis of quan-

titative analysis. Strangely, the dependency theorists have objected
to this demand and have considered measurement of variables as
irrelevant. Indeed, some have suggested that measurement is
irrelevant to a dialectical analysis. It is considered enough that there
should be strong categories to render clear the relations as a given
structural situation. Like some Marxists, the dependency theorists
also believe that structural interpretation is itself empirical evaluation.

This attitude expresses a disturbing degree of intellectual arro-
gance. It is also self-impoverishing as far as the refinement of the
theory itself is concerned. Philip O'Brien has rightly accused dependency theorists of circularity and of being victims of their own
circular argument. According to him, the dependency theories'
definition is that dependent countries are those which lack the
capacity for autonomous growth and they lack this because their
structures are dependent ones. This circular reasoning is not very
helpful.

Finally, it is not only bad theory but a definite method of disin-
formation to explain the plight of the LDCs in terms of the role of
their bourgeoisie only, which remains subservient to the political or
military elite. Besides, there is no dependency theory which can
identify the role of the bourgeoisie which is permanently half-
autonomous and half-comprador, just as there is no Marxist theory
which can satisfactorily explain the embourgeoisment of the working classes in the ADCs. There can be nothing more false than
dismissing ideology as false consciousness.

II

The general critique of the dependency theory given in the preceding pages does not in any way take away the analytical force of the
theory. What we hope to draw attention to is: (i) the inadequacy of
the theory and, more significantly, (ii) the absence of policy prescription. Dependency theorists have not been able to suggest what
the LDCs, their ruling or non-ruling elites or their masses, should
undertake to do within or outside the general framework of one or
the other theory of imperialism. So long as the ruling elites of the
LDCs are tied to those of the ADCs and the two work together
through their government representatives in all international fora,
no serious policy prescription can emerge from the dependency
theory. The suggestion that the world can be polarized on the basis
of joint class-state action nationally and internationally is a roman-

tic illusion. Centres of the socialist world are themselves in crisis and with their tilt towards capitalism have little to contribute to international anti-imperialism, all the more so because the so-called two systems are now openly converging.

The interdependency character of dependency as well as dependency is accepted by the theorists of imperialism, and this makes both belong to the same class of theories. It is true that some kind of relations will always exist between nations but the question is whether these relations allow the majority of nations, as grouped into ADCs and LDCs at present, to decisively influence global decisions. The dependency theory assumes a strong relationship between the two, whereas Darwinism assumes very weak relations. Indeed, dependency by its very name suggests a certain kind of mutuality, just as all theories of imperialism make such an assumption.

Probably the above view has been most explicitly stated by Hopkins and Wallerstein:

> There is one last matter to mention here, in concluding this section and drawing this chapter to a close. To repeat a general point, there has been an overall secular growth in the dependency of sovereignties on one another through the interstate system and in the dependence of production processes on one another through the axial division of labor. Analogously, there has been, for each of the two great revolutionary movements of the modern world-system, a sort of secular growth within each in the dependence on one another of the successively joined, long-term struggles constituting each movement.[4]

According to Dos Santos,

> by dependence we mean a situation in which the economy of certain countries is conditioned by the development and expansion of another economy to which the former is subjected. The relation of interdependence between two or more economies, and between these and world trade, assumes the form of dependence with some countries (the dominant ones)

[4] Terence K. Hopkins, Immanuel Wallerstein, *World Systems Analysis Theory and Methodology*, Sage Publications, p. 139.

can expand and can be self-starting, while other countries (the dependent ones) can do this only as a reflection of that expansion.[5]

The dependency theorists, particularly those of the Warren School, have argued that in view of low capital accumulation the LDCs, the periphery, would need capital from the ADCs, i.e., the centre. Indeed, they seem to suggest, in respect of the frontline states of Africa, that:

capital investments [in this case, capital investments from South Africa] are pre-requisites to the development of the productive forces, a necessary requirement for socialism. Such an analysis merges with the IMF/World Bank theories, of economic take-off, increased cash crop production and thus necessitates clear analysis in order to raise the question of the prospect for capitalist development in Africa.[6]

This position is one in which dependency and interdependence explicitly converge.

Other aspects on which dependency puts a strong emphasis, such as inequalities, exploitation or domination, cannot even be defined without assuming a strong interdependency. To quote Santos again:

this system is reproduced as a dependent one when it repro-duces a productive system whose development is limited by those world relations which necessarily lead to the develop-ment of only certain economic sectors, to trade under unequal conditions, to imposition of relations of super-exploitation of domestic labour force.[7]

This brings us to the question of Darwinism vs Dependency.

[5] Quoted by Makinlay and Little in *Global Problems and World Order*, S.S. Syndicate, New Delhi, pp. 132–33.

[6] Campbell Honae, 'War Reconstruction and Dependence in Mozambique', Two, October 1984.

[7] Ibid., McKinlay and Little, op. cit., p. 226.

III

Darwinism does not reject the theory of imperialism or neo-colonialism. It pushes itself to the farthest or highest stage of imperialism which carries on the old type of exploitation but does not live off it. A few imperialist nations rule the world, politically, militarily, economically and even culturally, by integrating some nations and by dividing and 'de-integrating' others. One critical aspect of the new situation of 'de-integrating' is that there is little chance of global depression, even of global recession. Dependency theorists accept the possibility of depression almost as a matter of faith. There may be serious problems of adjustments within the ADCs and LDCs, and there may be serious exploitation through internal colonialism, but there is no likelihood of a repitition of the thirties. One reason is that whereas global trade is of little over three trillion dollars, financial transactions amount to six hundred trillion, almost all carried within the ADCs. Financial Darwinism is one of the many mechanisms by which the global crisis is contained. The Wall Street crash of 1987 was so quickly reversed that it made nonsense of the global crisis theory.

An incident that happened in 1984 threw light on the new capabilities that global capitalism had developed. In 1984, when the debt bomb almost went off, the US Continental Illinois National Bank and Trust Co. was about to go bust. The bank was saved by a massive and unprecedented financial package of 7.5 billion dollars that was put up by the US government in complete coordination with the Federal Deposit Insurance Corporation. By taking that step President Reagan and the US Administration gave notice to put all believers in global depression that come what may there would be no repeat of 1929–31. There would be no 1929 no matter how strong was the boom in the US economy, so long as it was accompanied by high interest rates. There would be no 1931 either. President Reagan allowed more than 500 smaller banks to disappear but when it came to meeting the collapse of the eighth largest US bank, he stepped in to save it. The Continental Illinois was nationalized, something which no Republican govenment has ever done or was expected to do.[8]

The so-called intra-ADC crises have turned out to be no more

---

[8] *International Harold Tribune,* 25 Sept. 1984.

than large or small adjustment problems. The US-EEC or Japan-EDC trade problems, although not always easy to manage, are being tackled through a variety of means, often by methods which violate the rules of the game set by the ADCs themselves or by the delibrate violation of principles of international organizations such as GATT. The main thrust is to ensure that there is no global crisis. In this, the west is accommodating the communist countries too so that their economies do not collapse. Hungary, Poland and GDR are now treated as part of the global G-7 plans for stability.

Darwinism explains the absence of global crisis because it focuses on accelerated integration with ADCs. If there is no global crisis, it is partly because the global economy is so divided. On the other hand, the trade cycle impact on the LDCs has further pushed them towards a new rupture from one recession to another in the ADCs but, more significantly, the corresponding net transfers of capital to compensate for trade and price losses too have been declining. This has been reflected most sharply during the seventies and the eighties. But the debt burden kept on increasing with decline in capital transfer.

One of the central themes of dependency theory is that the global economic crisis is the crisis of the international division of labour. There is an enormous difficulty in the definition of the term international division of labour. From Adam Smith to the present day the term has been variously defined. It has one meaning in terms of trade theory, another in terms of division of production, still another in terms of technology and productivity increase. What is called international division of labour is a peculiar Marxist problematic into which facts do not fit. What the dependency theorists forget is that Marx had also described manufacture based on division of labour as 'an assassination of the people' and conversion of labour into 'a crippled monstrosity'. The worst aspect of the theory is that it legitimizes the functions of both the victim and the victimizer while allowing the cultural elites of the LDCs to remain in theoretical limb.

The advanced countries, both capitalist and socialist, pursue their own theories and policies of international division of labour. Notwithstanding claims about vital differences, the basic paradigm is the same as desired by the theory of comparative costs, which is one version of the international division of labour. By definition the ADC economies are supposed to be capital-intensive and the LDCs labour-intensive. But as the structural changes taking place in the former are faster and different, the impact is quite startling. The exports of ADCs to LDCs are now highly labour-intensive though labour is highly skilled, while the exports of low-labour skills have disappeared. On the other hand, the modern sectors—the new growth sectors—in the LDCs have turned into capital-intensive sectors through transfer of technology, multi-nationals and foreign management. But, these goods are not competitive.

One of the reasons for the low rate of growth of LDCs' export has been low productivity and technological backwardness. Notwithstanding the openness for technological imports that have been allowed under a policy of liberalization, export growth has remained modest. It is not possible for the LDCs to compete successfully in old products. For the creation of new products they do not have a technological base.

Several industries have shown a long-term declining cost curve either due to economies of scale or due to a downward shift of the curve itself due to technological improvements. Therefore, in the LDCs efforts to push up exports artificially and without strengthening the capital and technological base and without focusing on product life cycle comprehending product changes over time are not going to fructify.

All this has created new structural contradictions and ruptures within the LDC economies. In fact there is a double rupture. As trade relations developed between two sets of nations and emphasis shifted to the export of manufactures, some countries like South Korea, Japan and Taiwan, managed it well. But others failed miserably and when they were getting to manage somewhat better, the ADCs raised protection walls. Thus the whole theory of international division of labour which was to integrate the global economy simply helped to rupture it.

Dependency was the result of functions of markets for commodities, capital and labour power and technological transfers. Two clear conclusions may be drawn: (1) that the economic development of the LDCs is no longer as useful as it was for the ADCs; the backward world had always represented the indispensable hinterland of the highly developed west but that situation too is now resulting in diminishing returns; (2) that the development of the developed world itself has become inimical to the interests of the poor nations and although, in the short run the growth of developed countries may generate demand for the products of developing countries, in the long run the structural economic relations between the two tend to attenuate, largely due to the widening technological gap and changes in demand patterns.

This attenuation, or move towards Darwinism or rupture, finds its expression in a strange paradox. Whereas everybody is talking of interdependence, the situation on the ground is more of economic dualism, which is another way of defining rupture. As Streeten concludes: 'The integration of the upper classes of developing into the international system has created "national dualism" which sometimes leads to a call for nationalism on the one side and against it on the other.'[9]

This rupture, indeed, is the result of a stronger national economic ethos in the ADCs than in the LDCs. This attitude is a reflection of the well-established principle that equal treatment of unequals is not a principle of justice or democracy, a principle which was the very basis of the creation of the welfare state in the ADCs. The non-recognition of this principle cannot but cause rupture or disintegration. To say, as it is often said, that moral imperatives belong to individuals and not to states is the very basis of the international theory of rupture, both of values and economics.

Of course, the LDCs, by insisting on national sovereignty of natural resources, have themselves opted for the rupture. Except for oil and a few others, most of the natural resources of the world are located in the ADCs. The demand should have been to have a common pool of natural resources, capital and technology, particularly because the last two are overtaking the first. Most significantly, the few LDCs which possess natural resources such as oil, have rendered bankrupt the rest of the poor nations. The ADCs have been able to shift the burden of oil prices to the LDCs one way or another. Only OPEC is rich and it has adopted an even more unsympathetic attitude to other LDCs than the ADCs have done. The international debt trap was the result of an open conspiracy between the OPEC and the ADCs. Indeed, the OPEC no longer belongs to the LDC group of nations and have been fully co-opted by the ADCs. Consequently, they are not prepared 'to transfer the additional resources as the South is not prepared to give necessary undertaking'.[10]

---

[9] Paul Streeten, in *Economic Theory and New World Order*, (ed.) H.W. Singer and others, Ashish publishing, New Delhi, 1987, p. 5.

[10] P. Streeten, ibid., p. 29.

What has happened to the so-called North-South dialogue, or for that matter to the South-South dialogue, is instructive. Except for some initial enthusiasm the whole thing has turned out to be a damp squib, if not a fraudulent exercise. In 1974 the UN General Assembly passed a resolution on the subject which stated that NIEO is to be based on 'Equity, sovereign equality, common interest and cooperation among all the States, irrespective of their social and economic system, which shall correct inequitable and regress existing injustices'. At best, that statement was a pious hope; at worst, it was fraudulent and a cover-up. No wonder, the North openly refused to accept that model of it which would have meant a move towards a truly interdependent world based on morality
and sacrifice. To the North, the distinction between the old and the new orders was that between the Bretton Woods system and the one that came after it. Neither made any difference to the South. The old and new orders are methods of integration within the ADCs, what H.W. Singer has called the 'convergence' of the ADCs.

Whether it was trade with the advanced capitalist economies or the socialist economies, the result for the LDCs was increasing structural disproportions. At the face of it the ADCs aimed at liberalizing trade in general but the net result of expanding international trade regimes was to restrict the growth of the LDCs even if their imports and exports increased. This was due to a variety of factors such as decline in the terms of trade, debt service burden or uncertainties, shifts in sectoral production or exports, restrictions on trade, etc. The LDCs remain in disequilibrium as a result of the attempts of the ADCs to create their own equilibrium. There is no particular force in the global correlation between increase in trade and that in growth rate, though fluctuations in the economy due to changes in trade are enormous. Whereas the share of the external factor in the economic development of the LDCs, i.e. internationalization as distinguished from interdependence, has increased, the rate of development as well as the share in trade have refused to go up. In fact, the larger the internationalization, the smaller is the growth rate in many LDCs. This proves the truth of both Darwinism and dependency theories, but only partly, because the role of the LDCs in the development of the ADCs has correspondingly declined. The paradoxical situation can be defined as one of *ruptured dependence*. Import-oriented import substitution (India and Mexico) as opposed to autonomous or export-oriented import substitution (South Korea) ensured ruptured dependencies.

The structural changes within the economies of the ADCs point towards another kind of rupture also. They have been attempting for two decades to shut out raw materials from the LDCs by (i) finding non-natural substitutes, (ii) changing the material intensity of output, and (iii) changing the demand pattern.

When stripped of the rhetoric, the ADCs' position on North-South relations is as follows:

> The overall politico-economic 'frame of reference' which Northern policy-makers employ seems to rest, implicitly, upon the views that: (i) the global economy, if run on a more or less laissez-faire basis, under the aegis of the revised Bretton Woods institutions and the GATT, functions reasonably effectively and requires no further 'global management' except when special circumstances may require; (ii) the South is not a sufficiently important component of the global economy for it to play any greater role in global decision-making than it now does; (iii) the most important influences upon Northern welfare are those which are determined by North/North (including East/West) agreements or disputes; and (iv) the South can and should, therefore, be handled—as distribution is handled in traditional market theory—as a separate matter for independent bargaining over distribution, with the clear presumption that how much the Southern 'clients' receive is a matter for the Northern 'patrons' discretion.[11]

The multinationals, one would have expected, would erode Darwinism by integrating all economies. But in practice they have done the opposite. They have set up subsidiaries and collaborative projects in the LDCs and this very process leads to Darwinism within the LDCs. Non-collaborative industries are fast disappearing, leading to economic dualism. The multinationals use internal planning and processes to transfer costs to the LDCs' major business houses. In reality, the multinationals integrate the LDCs' major business houses with those from the ADCs. International financial flows are the other instrument for keeping this integra-

[11] Gerald K. Helleiner, in *Economic Theory and New World Order*, op.cit., pp. 60–61.

tion. The rest of the economy is denied capital and financial inputs.

Another blow to the old theories came from the fusion of capital within the ADCs. Trade economists have recognized that the international fusion of capital has proceeded far enough to replace a large number of imperialist superpowers. But they do not carry the argument further. They do not see the Darwinist implications of their own position. Darwinism clearly explains multilateral imperialism. Sometimes, the phrase 'unequal' interests is used to show technological differences but it is not very helpful. Multilateral or pluralist imperialist is the latest phase of balanced rivalries, and cooperation among various imperialist alliances are examples more of cooperation than rivalry. Giant nations, the US, USSR and China became rivals and by their size and resources also expansionist. But whether rivals or friends they are all pushing out nations of the South from the global system as far as possible.

Non-economists have their own version of these two approaches. Political scientists and sociologists point out the neglect by economists of the political and social factors, particularly the political and military domination by a small group of nations of the rest. Their theories prove that even if the developing countries industrialized and did not simply produce primary goods, the ADCs would be able to combine the widening gaps in trade, finance and technology and political advantages to maintain their hold. The rise of multinationals, monopoly of R&D and of weapon systems, and more subtle control of education, health and other aspects of the life of poor nations, inevitably creates a political structure of LDCs marginalization through dominance.

In political writings there is some mention, though not a serious analysis, of the international political anarchy and political fracturing as distinguished from economic fracturing. The two are related, but the argument leaves out the cause and effect relations. Generally, those who focus on political disorder have in view the threat of nuclear war, which exists, but is seldom taken seriously by those who possess the weapons. Robin Lukham sums up the argument thus:

> It is characteristic of political rhetoric that people talk of international order when what stares in the face is anarchy. The world is passing through a crisis the like of which it has not known since World War II. The anarchy of capitalism has plunged it into global economic crisis. At the same time

fracturing of the international political order has already brought wars to the Third World. The ultimate form of anarchy would be nuclear war.

Though Lukham's concern is with recession he observes nevertheless:

> The two major dimensions of the crisis, the recession in capitalism and the fracturing of the international political order, cannot be analysed separately. It is symptomatic of our present condition that they are kept apart both in academic discourse and in day-to-day business of international relations.[12]

Tragically, the Dependency theory which began as a theory of anti-imperialist resistance has been reduced to a new normative theory advocating radical dependence.

---

[12] Robin Lukham, 'Militarization and the New International Anarchy', Two, April 1984.

THEORY AND CRITICISM
OF INTERDEPENDENCE

In this chapter I propose to sketch, rather briefly, and provide a critique of the theory of interdependence. Until Gorbachev's rise to power and deepening crisis of communist economies, interdependence was never seriously analysed by Marxists even though the capitalist world had woven in itself the principle of interdependence, one version of which was concealed imperialism. Marxists, including dependency theorists, did not give it enough exposure as a model of imperialism. The real difficulty is that there is no single universally accepted model of either interdependence or imperialism. The purpose here is to show how inter-state relations, multilateral regimes, multinationals, etc., and their policy components and instrumentalities can succeed either by exploitation or by pushing many LDCs further towards Darwinism. The Brandt Commission, the OECD, the Group-77 and the South Commission are the chief purveyors of interdependence. Exploitation has reached such limits that no further squeeze is possible. Only the Darwinist structure seems possible within the present order. The tragedy is that the victim is cooperating with the victimiser in this.

The political economy of interdependence originated from Smith and Ricardo, but the modern theory, as a grand design, was launched by the Bretton Woods Conference in 1945 and reinforced by the USAdministration from the early 1960s. It had four objectives: (i) sharing nuclear forces with Europe in order to avoid the fragmentation and compartmentalization of the NATO powers, as was explained by McNamara; (ii) liberalizing trade in order to optimize economic advantages for the ADCs; (iii) integrating the third world with the liberal capitalist part of the world economy;

and (iv) eliminating the communist world from the global economic order.

Besides Neoclassicists, there were radical proponents of the interdependence theory who claimed to be left-liberals or left-Keynesians. Tinbergin, Prebisch, Kaldor, the Pearson Commission, the Brandt Commission, and several others are well known for their support of the model of interdependence. They advocated, through the UN agencies, particularly UNCTAD, the opening of markets of the ADCs for goods of the LDCs, transfer of technology, creation of commodity funds in order to protect the terms of the trade of LDCs and foreign aid, etc. It is most significant that both the first and second world nations fully subscribed to the idea of interdependence, though from different perspectives. Washington and Moscow and the international bodies which they dominated echoed the same sentiments even when engaged in cold war and economic sanctions. Interdependence is Moscow's first priority today.

Interdependence may be given either a subjective or an objective definition. Subjectively, interdependence is supposed to reflect global consensus and awareness about economic, societal, ecological and other issues, a recognition of the humanity of man, i.e., the mutuality of the interests of humanity as a whole and a shared common destiny woven into a global network of relations. Objectively, interdependence is seen in expanded world trade and financial transactions, technology transfers knitting together the world through fast developing communications, global linkages between growth rates, employment, inflation, trade, etc., pollution of water and air by one country transferring its problems to another.

The basic rationale and theories of one world economy deserve to be stated clearly because these are built around theories of interdependence. The most important statement made is that the earth has rapidly dwindled to a small place with humanity crowding in on it. The idea of human development and human consciousness has become popular. Human beings require all-round development as an integrated whole.

The development of modern communications, media, and transport have not merely shrunk the globe but have linked the remotest parts of the world, so much so that no place on the earth is beyond a day's distance from another and in a few minutes any one man can talk to any other. Events of historial significance have taken place in recent years to affect the future of the whole mankind, though not always in such a way as to arouse the interest of world public opinion towards one world.

In terms of development, it is stated loudly that prosperity is becoming indivisible and that even the rich countries will not be able to survive in the long run in the ocean of misery. In other words, economic development has become a matter of international responsibility. Mankind has opened up immense natural resources and invented technologies either to improve the welfare of nations or to destroy peoples' lives and both have become inseparable parts of development. Since natural resources are unevenly distributed among nations, there is an indispensable dependence of one population on another; nations of the world have to carry on as if they belong to one family, with its members owning different but complementary resources.

The most important theory that evolved from the aforementioned facts is that of the international division of labour, as analysed in the previous chapter. International exchange of commodities and services, including the exchange of intellectual products, flow from this theory to set the basis of an emerging one world. The division of labour creates a sort of dependence among units participating in it, be they nations or groups, which requires movement of goods, capital and services across boundaries. In fact in many ways there is no essential difference between economic movements within a single country and between countries, if one goes by the principle of international division of labour. Marxist and neoclassical economists are one in saying that the international division of labour is the highest form of the division of labour among specialized units working in specific systems of various sovereign countries. Briefly, the formation and maintenance of the international division of labour requires deep cooperation and harmonization of the interests of various nations.

Ironically, the so-called interdependence of the sovereign nations within a single world economy is quite tortuous, if not divisive. Although it mainly relates to international commodity exchange, international services, manpower migration, capital flows, worldwide specialized production, increasing international flow of intellectual property and so on, there are also non-economic aspects of interdependence, such as war. The latter do not concern us here.

Probably the most explicit expression of interdependence is the role of expanding international trade. Trade is justified on account of efficiency, welfare, factor price equalization, complementarities, easing of transport, and above all for reasons of economic development.

Behind trade and interdependence lies the principle of accumulation of capital which accrues from exploitation of profitable opportunities for investment resources in the creation of capital of different types. Capital accumulation is the central lever of growth and development which creates incomes, enlarges markets and provides opportunities for specialization. Profit and capital accumulation are parts of integrated world development and have self-reinforcing and agglomerating qualities. In an autarkic situation, capital accumulation will be much less, it is argued, although every fast accumulating country has, in some measure or the other, relied on protectionism. But phases of liberalization and protectionism have not stopped the process of global integration.

The historical view of international economic relations presented in the form of stages of development or other theories also suggests a continuous movement towards global integration through the expansion of the global market and opening up of investment opportunities. Rostow's theory of take-off, Myrdal's cumulative circular causation, Peroux's *poles de croissance*, and above all, Marx's theory of stages of historical transformation, all assume that economic development inevitably tends to spread out from the country of origin to the rest of the world, as a consequence of the pursuit of profit, welfare or even sheer fancy. Interdependence is a dynamic historical process.

The tremendous growth of international monetary institutions and the spread of multi-billion transactions taking place daily all over the world help in the adjustment of the process towards achieving the dynamic efficiency of the international economic order. Just as the shift from the barter economy to the money economy improved efficiency, the complex growth of the international monetary system has helped trade to grow, which in turn, has helped integrate global economic activities, particularly consumption and investment.

It is firmly believed that notwithstanding all the restrictions, protection walls, quota barriers, and economic nationalism, which are the policy instruments of modern nation states, there is something like Adam Smith's invisible hand also working in the international system which makes the world move towards a single market.

Although theories of interdependence are not blind to the fact that the global system is as much conflictual as cooperative, they firmly believe that, in the long run, notwithstanding all wars and conflicts, the idea of interdependence has to be normatively exploited. There is no inevitability towards interdependence and even if there are strong forces working towards integration, the opposite forces are also there. In her book, *The Rich Nations and the Poor Nations*, economist Barbara Ward has said, 'History teaches us that changes of such amplitude have sometimes been brought about through dialogue and cooperation, sometimes by a direct and violent confrontation, but most often by a mixture of confrontation and cooperation.' Those who benefit from a system tend to be stubborn in refusing to make changes. But others believe that nothing will change without a total overturn. 'When this stage of polarization is reached', adds Barbara Ward, 'dialogue is impossible and violence becomes inevitable, unless a way is found to go beyond the stage of egoism and to discover together a community of interest.'[1]

The basic framework of the model is that since the end of World War II, and more particularly recently, the global system has been divided between economic, security and cultural relations: three streams sometimes running parallel with different structures but often intermeshed with one another. Although the overall name given to this global system is interdependence, the analysis given here would show that this interdependence is strong in some relations and fake in others, leaving the model indeterminate. The only determinancy is that the global power elite finds this indeterminacy necessary for its determinate power.

It is important to note that European nationalism subscribed to global interdependence with a lot of caution. It subscribed to regional as against global interdependence. De Gaulle thought that too much interdependence between Europe and the US would lead to the domination of Europe by the US. The European Left feared interdependence from the other angle: it may curtail Europe's independence in foreign policy vis-à-vis the superpowers and the third world. Paradoxically, the Europeans wanted the US nuclear umbrella in order not to incur the cost of defence, but also wanted independence in foreign policy even in cases which hurt US interests as understood by the US. There are scores of cases which illustrate European defiance of the US. However, ultimately, a

[1] Barbara Ward, *The Rich Nations and the Poor Nations*, New York, Norton, 1972.

single global order came to be seen by all ADC regional and other international regimes. By 1992 EEC would have launched a new model of economic interdependence. No one is being allowed to challenge the new order.

It is claimed by the ADC economists that the world was better integrated before World War II under conditions of fixed exchanges, balanced budget policies, etc. Keynes had laid the theoretical basis for this disintegration of the global system. Imperialism was a factor of global economic integration.

Interdependence has been the great liberal slogan of the ADCs in the post-Keynesian era, but each ADC twisted it in its own favour. The Europeans welcome trade surplus with the US resulting from its high growth rate, but criticize the US for other inevitable consequences of the growth. Notwithstanding the noises made about supply side economics, high growth rate is attributable to budget deficits. But Europeans denounce budget deficits as they keep interest rates high which, in turn, drain away European investment funds to the US, though this process ensures against recession. But high interest rates and budget deficits together made the dollar strong and have produced the worst ever balance of trade deficit from which Europe and Japan have largely benefited. Obviously, the Europeans want to have their cake and eat it too.

They brazenly hold contradictory positions and treat the LDCs with disdain. Now they say: There are two opposite forces at work. National integration contributes to international disintegration, but the rejection of irrational constraints by each state also produces global irrationality. A new kind of integration has taken place, i.e., integration of the upper classes of the developing countries into the international system. This is the only integration or interdependence for the LDCs. For the ADCs, interdependence, which means greater trade, investments and profits, is always counterbalanced by interests demanding protectionism and raising the slogan of economic nationalism. The labour and smokestack industries demand protection while the multinationals promote interdependence. Contrary to economists' predictions, the liberal economic order faced no threat from parochialism as it balanced the disadvantages of unrestricted interdependence which otherwise hurt the LDCs and even some of the smaller developed nations.

II

Darwinism stands poles apart from the theory of economic interdependence. Aspects other than economics, such as culture, politics and security, sometimes blur the sharp division, but in economics the choices are limited for the LDCs. My central thesis is that contrary to the normal general impression, the global system is not only not interdependent in economic relations, but it is ruptured and increasingly subject to international economic Darwinism.

On the other hand, for purposes of security and in the face of the nuclear threat the world is easily treated as one and fully interdependent. Yet the concept of common global security has generated many more wars among the LDCs than ever before even though this interdependence is acting as a deterrent to nuclear war. Finally, it is in the cultural field that interdependence in the form of absolute dependence is complete. The dependency theorists are looking on the wrong side of the telescope; it is in the cultural field that dependency is complete and it is weakest in the economic field. In the latter, as discussed in the preceding chapters, what is happening is the growing rupture and threat of total marginalization of a large number of weak economies of the LDCs.

The LDCs have been faced at once with the problems of national integration, nation-building and seeking viable membership of the global order. Their attempts in this regard have been viewed suspiciously as a stumbling block in the way of creating a new order of interdependence. That is no nonsense, as it is an inevitable form of neo-imperialism. It is already admitted that the ruling classes of the LDCs are fully integrated with the ADCs as part of this neo-imperialism. Besides, the ADCs have shown no less preference for their own nationalism except when acting as a member of a bloc of nations. What is more true is that the cohesive integration or interdependence of the LDCs or South has been frustrated not only by their dependence on the ADCs but the latter's formation into various blocs which are getting increasingly integrated both for economic and security purposes. Therefore, the best chance of interdependence is between blocs of ADCs and industrialized LDCs, notwithstanding the noises made by the Non-aligned movement, Group-77 and other such tub-thumping organizations. The relevant and dominating international regimes all belong to the ADCs. The hetrogeneity and lack of cohesion among the LDCs are an irrefutable empirical evidence against the theory of interdependence. In fact, what is called economic dualism of the global economic system is a clear negation of interdependence.

There is national capitalism; there is an international capitalist system. There is national socialism; there is an international socialist system. Washington and Moscow are their respective centres. The latter is showing signs of disintegration but it is an intra-ADC adjustment as all East Europeans are overanxious to join the EEC. Both survived by expanding their spheres of influence, but all in the name of security. However, the expansion took place mostly in the third world. All the conflicts between the two systems of superpowers have been fought in Asia or Africa. Cold war, an expression of negative global consciousness, was translated into many hot wars, but not on the soils of the capitalist or developed European socialist nations. When the struggle is reduced to creating zones of influence, there can be no genuine global consciousness of interdependence or if it is there, it is certainly based on exploitation. Be it détente or cold war, in each case the LDCs are pushed around and ultimately pushed out.

It is very clear that but for a few exceptions, most LDCs are condemned to live in poverty, squalor and elite vulgarity as an inevitable part of this interdependence. In this ADCs and LDCs division, there is no scope for global or world consciousness or equality. New international capitalism is rapidly absorbing international socialism through its financial labryinth. Socialist countries owe more than 120 billion dollars to capitalist states or their financial institutions. Despite their conflicts, they are covering vast areas of cooperation. Ironically, the more they cooperate, the more global consciousness is weakened.

In order to rationalize and sustain the aforementioned order, Frances Steward and Paul Streeten have given interdependence four functions: first, the ADCs' balance of payments surplus is to be invested in the LDCs; second, the existence of financial institutions to invest these surpluses; third, the existence in ADCs of industries that produce and sell capital goods needed for development; fourth, military power to back the economic power derived from the previous three functions.[2]

The above is a fair, honest statement of the ADCs' position of dominance as it is divorced from all the rhetoric of a brave new

[2] H.W. Singer and others (eds.,) *Economic Theory and New World Order*, Ashish, New Delhi, 1987, Chap. II.

world. The problems of markets for the goods of LDCs in the markets of ADCs, self-reliance, income inequalities are all secondary. Other secondary issues listed are energy, pollution, stagflation, unemployment, etc. This definition of the NIEO is a model to which existing practices and policies conform, as against the utopian model or models demanded by the LDCs. It is, in plain words, a clear statement of *dependent interdependence*.

The Brandt Commission took a lofty view of interdependence and to fill the void, made technology the chief determinant. It wrote,

> We must do away with the idea that our problems exist only because there are 'developed' countries and countries which want to be 'developed'. After all, the technological and economic development process in the North has not yet come to an end, and there is a fierce discussion about how to progress from here—with different technologies, with a less wasteful way of life.[3]

Although the Brandt Commission drew attention to the unpromising and unacceptable aspects of the debate before the 1980s, its emphasis was largely on charity and economy. It never asked for a debate on structures. The report fell short of doing what it promised. Charity is a camouflage for non-mutuality of benefits. The report came at a time when the cold war was at its height, the arms race at its fastest and the sale of arms to the third world at its biggest. It was a diversionary tactic away from security issues and third world wars. No wonder the report said, 'The relationship between armament and development is still very much in the dark.'[4]

Interdependence as explained by its advocates in a world of great unequals, the exploited and exploiters, etc., is more like an animal game, as is suggested by Lester Thorou. According to him, the economic problem is essentially like that of the wolves and the caribus. If the wolves eat all caribus, the wolves will also vanish. Conversely, if the wolves vanish, the caribus survive for a time but eventually their ranks become too large and they die for lack of food.[5]

[3] *North-South*, Pan Books, London, 1980, pp. 23-24.
[4] Ibid., p. 13.
[5] Ravi Batra, *The Great Depression of 1990*, Simon & Schuster, New York, 1987, p. 15.

III

Interdependence and LDCs: A Critique

In the earlier chapter, data was presented on trade, production technology and financial transfers to show how (i) most LDCs are being Darwinized and not being treated under any well-defined concept or model of interdependence; (ii) how the ADCs are fast integrating themselves multilaterally through trade, investment and technological cooperation; and (iii) how competition among the ADCs has become the dynamic force for this integration. The theory of International Economic Darwinism is the direct antithesis of the theory of interdependence.

The situation of an LDC is seen in the light of three issues or possibilities. They are: economic sovereignty, autonomy and interdependence. Sovereignty implies the right and ability to make decisions affecting a country's political economy in both domestic and international arenas. Autonomy is the actual ability to manage the domestic economy in accordance with a pattern of growth and welfare which corresponds to policy makers' requisites for maintaining sovereignty and legitimacy.[6] For instance, if a country can conveniently meet external economic constraints and demands from its own resources over the long run, that country is said to enjoy autonomy. True interdependence, as distinguished from dependence or false interdependence, is the capacity to avoid both negative and zero sum economic relations and to gain a substantial part of positive gains from trade, capital, services, etc.

Interdependence is also the capacity to influence the economic behaviour of other nations or international organizations. The absence of that ability is called the vulnerability of a nation or state which is defined as the opportunity cost to an action of forging relations. Although in economic literature unequal relations are either called dependency or asymmetry of relations, the dynamic of interdependence to change the asymmetry and dependence is part of it. For instance, the fact that the superpowers can destroy one another through the use of nuclear weapons and also destroy the rest of the world is a stark example of global interdependence although this interdependence, for policy purposes, also rules out role for most nations which are non-nuclear.

[6] David Moses, 'Mexico's Challenges', *Third World Quarterly*, July 1987.

Interdependence itself can lead to destabilization of policies. For instance, when it comes to nations, they are becoming more interdependent in terms of their economic welfare and trade sanctions have become a permanent weapon for dealing with political and military adversaries. The oil embargo that was imposed during the Arab-Israel war in 1973 seriously affected the interdependence of various nations. The US restriction on grain sales to the Soviet Union after the invasion of Afghanistan and sanctions against Poland after the imposition of martial law were cases of economic interdependence being misused for political blackmail and military purposes. Political and military interdependence can be interpreted in many different ways.

Paul Streeten questions interdependence in another way: 'Coexistence in an interdependent world can give rise to the production of "goods"; but it can also give rise to the production of "bads", which have to be combated by "antibads". The exploration of areas of joint action for "antibads" may be even more important than the search for "goods".'[7]

Technically, interdependence is used as an economic concept. In reality, it is used in every field of relations between nations. Nations arrive at arrangements by means of which they become interdependent in security, political and communication areas, etc. The problem is that economic and non-economic interdependence can have both a positive and a negative impact on each other. If interdependence is used for political or military subjugation of a small nation by a big one, it remains a kind of interdependence as were the whole series of imperialist systems of the past. Most importantly, the relations between the US and the USSR seriously affect economic and political interdependent sub-systems everywhere.

The present global system rests on another assumption in order to establish a common society. Such issues as choice of government relations between government and citizens and the determination of national interests and foreign policies are uniformly viewed as matters of domestic jurisdiction. Of course, the assumption is false, because small and medium nations are unable to exercise such jurisdiction and, explicitly or implicitly, their decisions are interfered with. However, the assumption undermines the value system on which a new world can be based. The assumption implies the

[7] Paul Streeten, *Economic Theory and New World Order*, p. 33

coexistence of democratic and autocratic regimes as well as of very poor and very rich nations. The assumption moves in even more absurd directions when the government of a nation can liquidate millions of innocent people and still remain a respectable member of the international community. The perversion of human values within the prevailing global system remains unchecked by international law and international organizations. Unless some method is developed by means of which values are clearly defined and respected by every nation, there will be no free international community.

On one issue, all the theories of interdependence, Darwinism and dependency converge. Over a range of subjects both Darwinism and dependency would describe interdependence as 'dependent interdependence'. It is defined as a set of relations by which the ADCs keep control over the LDCs, irrespective of the fact whether resources and technology transfers are more or less. There is a definite pattern of domination. Sometimes it is called neo-colonialism, but this term lacks rigorous definition. Besides, neo-colonialism is rhetoric used by Marxists and the communist countries to denounce their capitalist counterparts as much as by third world populist dictators and corrupt power elites who rely on radical rhetorics to safeguard their power. However, a jump from domination to 'turning out of the system' marks the vital difference between the two. Where one ends, the other begins.

Nations as economic entities either submit to the forces of global interdependence and integrate or try to insulate key sectors of the economy and let the rest be subject to interdependence and then try to negotiating for a *minimax* position of minimum cost and maximum benefit. Most LDCs have been obliged to submit themselves to interdependence. India, Mexico, Brazil and other middle economic powers attempted to insulate some sectors through import substitution. China insulated the entire economy for a long time before going in for positive interdependence. Since it is global interdependence which distributes both costs and benefits by insulating, one can avoid the costs by participation in it, but the benefits are not always certain. Indeed, for most LDCs the benefits have been negative.

Like dependency theory, interdependence too claims to rest itself on the economic concept of international division of labour. Indeed there is more than one concept dating from Adam Smith to the present day. The Soviets used it so often to justify their theory of two systems or to buttress their foreign policy objectives and in so many ways that the original Marxist definition was twisted beyond recognition. The definition given by Gunder Frank is nearest to current reality and functions both the interdependent and dependency versions.

> There has been a radical shift in the international division of labour and the intersectoral division of labour, in which some lose out in a sort of world game of musical chairs. Particularly, the leaders lose out and others come to occupy their respective positions, and much of the battle is about the sharing out of the costs and the benefits of this major process of readjustment in the world economy. I submit that this process is largely beyond the capability of policy to either effect or even to stem the tide.[8]

Both imperialism and dependency are versions of and variations on interdependence. Exploiting nations always has deep interest in maintaining the position of the exploited just as imperialism had the need for the colonies. Not only can one not exist without the other, the dialectics and dynamics of their relations produce both conflict and cooperation on which the global order rests. Of course, normatively the two are mutually exclusive but if such a situation were to be obtained, the result will be either true interdependence or its complete disappearance.

The main rationale of old theories of imperialism was derived from the theories of division of labour, of capital accumulation, of declining domestic investment opportunities and hence the need to push towards the export of capital. In the long run, under capitalism, according to the classical theories of imperialism, it was unprofitable for an advanced capitalist country to invest at home in older industries. This view has already become anachronistic. Now, largely though not entirely, most of the capital flows, both short and long term, take place within the ADCs. Darwinism implies a small or even declining flow of capital flows to LDCs. Its corollary is that concentration and internationalization of capital also are relevant only for the ADCs. The international monopolies or multinationals are now forms of the ADCs' cooperating and

---

[8] A. Gunder Frank, 'World Economic Crisis and Policy Perspective in the Mid 1980s', in *Economic Theory and New World Order*, p. 511.

competing entities from which LDC firms producing the same goods are excluded. NATO, the Marshall Plan, Bretton Woods, the IMF, the World Bank and their respective strategies were designed not only to contain and isolate the Soviet Union but also to resist the demands of the LDCs. Thus, by working out its multinational strategy, US imperialism undertook to underwrite other capitalist states. This neo-imperialism is less competitive and more multilateral, which ironically laid the paradoxical basis for both interdependence and Darwinism.

From primitive to modern societies, two factors have played the key role of differentiation: technology and values. We cannot fail to see that be it interdependence, dependency or Darwinism, technology has become more important than most other factors put together. Technological changes are occurring so fast and are so disruptive or productive that almost every school of thought is being swept off its feet. Technology is creating an environment not only of great excitement but also of great uncertainty and instabi - lity. Adjustments, institutional and others, to technological forces are becoming more and more difficult. The technological changes of the last two decades have left many old problems unsolved while having created new ones.

By and large, the paradigm of interdependence dominated the debate about the rate of technological change and the rate of adjustment to the change. The crucial argument is that national efforts to adopt the changes have become insufficient and many international institutions of the inter-governmental variety too have become obsolete. Technological change is transcending national sovereignties and enthroning full interdependence. Things are not so simple, if only because the LDCs are generally kept out of the technological race. There is no open technological market.

A few significant developments deserve special mention. To begin with, one has to accept that technological progress is bewilderingly fast and all-encompassing. What one chip or a disk or a computer can do today is million times more powerful than what men and machines did even two or three decades ago. Technology has put the information revolution at the centre of the globe. But the issue that concerns us is how all this has influenced national economies, international trade and finance and control over resources. Michael Blumenthal, a very experienced expert says:

Technological change is also altering trade. In fact, for one who spent four long years in arduous negotiations to lower tariff barriers and increase world trade, it is a sobering thought that technological changes appear to be having a far greater impact on the nature and volume of international commerce than all the *trade* negotiations since the 1948 establishment of the GATT combined.[9]

Therefore, those who pin hope on negotiations must be warned. It is also dangerous to believe that negotiations on technology are knitting or integrating the whole world.

Like the global trading regimes, there are many technological regimes which not only control the allocation of resources but also determine the nature of resources. Besides, technology has become a system through which economic power is ultimately used.

Modern technological regimes are formed not by nations only, but also by economic organizations and interests on the one hand, and by scientists and technological experts on the other. Every nation tries to keep control over both because in the final analysis she finds that competitiveness and productivity depend upon control of technologies. The economic nationalism of the ADCs is most fiercely reflected in their national technological regimes. Even within an alliance system, secretiveness, jealousies and desire for appropriation in respect of technologies remain a critical barrier for further integration. Unlike international trading regimes such as GATT and other organizations, there is no international techno-logical trading regime. The day such a regime comes into being the monopoly of the control of a few powerful nations over the rest would be complete, and the globe would be fractured in every sense of the word. Before such a calamity comes down on us it is important that a more equitable, ecologically justifiable technologi-cal regime with spiritual dimensions be created right now. In the LDCs, the imperative is to both exploit ADCs' technologies and to keep those technologies out by which ADCs can control them.

In the field of international finance and stock market dealing, information and communication technology, where billions of international currencies and stocks are exchanged in seconds and moments, three or four ADC centres matter. New York, Tokyo,

[9] W.M. Blumenthel, 'The World Economy and Technical Change', *Foreign Affairs*, No. 3, 1988.

London and Bonn control the international markets. Outside these few markets practically little exists by way of these activities. The world is totally fractured financially between monopolies and non-entities. Control over communication and information technologies is helping to exclude the vast majority of nations from the global financial system. The international monetary system, whether in order or disorder, has been criticized by everybody because it has come to dominate international trade without creating stability in return for such domination. Ignoring the question of equity and fairness, two objections are clearcut: one concerns the effectiveness with which the system mediates between lenders and borrowers or between surplus and deficit countries; second, the institutions of international capital and money have so much interfered in economic relations among nations as to create increased volatility and uncertainty both in trade and capital markets. Volatility of exchange rates does affect LDC trade, as do other operations in the financial markets. These operations in turn produce more and not less exchange fluctuations.

There has been no consensus whether in the interests of interdependence exchange rates should be left floating or be managed. Nations often change their position on this question, depending on their current preferences. The important problem is that it is commodity transactions which determine the exchange rates rather than the rates determining the commodity transactions. The prevailing system of relations among national economies has raised concern among analysts that exchange rate volatility may reduce the volume of trade by making international transactions more risky and passing the burden to weaker economies.

Whatever the rules of the game for trade, those for currency exchange markets are always subject to government intervention. The idea of market-oriented rates has had very brief periods. From 1945 to even the 1970s the Bretton Woods era was an era of managed currencies. For the next fifteen years exchange rates were allowed to float, but within limits as fixed by the central banks of half a dozen advanced countries. For some years now the persistence of low growth rates, fear of inflation accompanied by wildly oscillating currencies, etc., has created new uncertainty. In 1985 in the Plaza Hotel Conference in New York, it was decided that governments should accept the responsibility of giving the market the lead. Subsequent conferences, particularly of February, 1987, at Louvre, of the big seven talked of exchange rate instability endan-

gering world economic prospects. In April 1987 at the IMF meeting
a commodity index was added to the list of indicators to be
watched. The Plaza and Louvre accords led to all agreeing first to
the lowering of the value of the dollar and then to stabilizing it with
government or central bank intervention. The row between Mrs
Thatcher and her finance minister Lawson led to the defeat of the
former in favour of managing currencies and not allowing the
pound to rise very much. The point is that there is no free market
as the protagonists of interdependence would like us to believe.

The burden of debt, which otherwise links ADCs and LDCs, is
producing negative results. What has happened in the last two or
three years in international banking circles has exposed the hollow-
ness of the claims of interdependence. When an LDC is in trouble,
the international banking system thinks of reducing, not increasing, the loans. It may be true that international loans have become
more risky, but that is a different question and should be dealt with
as a structural problem. To reduce loans at a time when interdependence demands more loans reveals the exploitative and divisive character of the international banking system.

The burden of interest rates is a problem by itself which transfers
resources from the poor to the rich. The continued maintenance of
high interest rates is a phenomenon which cannot be taken lightly
as just one aspect of international financial loaning. It definitely
means the transfer of resources back from poor countries to rich
countries. Just one percentage point increase in interest rates means
a minimum flow-back into the developed countries of something
like 4 billion dollars. In fact, since 1977–78, when interest rates
started moving up, this burden has doubled and the poor developing countries have been paying to the developed countries something like 30 billion dollars a year. Now, globally, there is a general
reverse transfer of resources. Interdependence could not have been
more perverse.

Several other developments, which superficially may suggest
that the world is getting more interdependent, conceal the fact that
world is getting more fractured. I will cite a few cases.

Trade in raw material of the LDCs, which forms one of the pillars
of interdependence, is facing competition from substitutes created
by technology, or facing a declining market because of structural
changes in the economies of the ADCs. Materials like copper, tin,
aluminium, nickel, even old bloc steel, face fierce competition,
leaving a devasting impact on the economies of the producing

countries. The competitive strength of the latter has dwindled and is likely to go down further as new technologies keep substituting these materials. Commodity-producing LDCs are joining the international ghetto, not an interdependent system.

The combined effect of electronics, biotechnology, genetics, etc. have reversed the old division between surplus and deficit or food and raw material producing and consuming nations. The ADCs are now surplus producers of food and many poor nations are living on the margin of starvation as they have ruined old agriculture without the benefit of new technologies. Some LDCs have so ruined their agriculture by resorting to commercial crops that they do not have the economic power to buy food. These are the days of small international charities to save the starving in order that they can remain alive as destitutes and thus maintain the ghetto.

Some of the ADCs, particularly USA and Britain, have been going through internal de-industrialization. Indeed the share of manufacturing in these economies has persistently declined. Had this adjustment been the result of a concession to LDCs for the vacation of certain industries for the latter's benefit, one would have given credence to the NIEO. In fact, the result has been quite the opposite. Internal de-industrialization has led to their raising new protection walls against the imports from the LDCs. Adjustments in domestic industries in the ADCs caused by the rise of new trading regimes give advantage to those who have pushed themselves ahead in productivity increases. From the sixties onwards, productivity in Western Europe (excluding Britain) was twice that of USA, and of Japan twice that of Western Europe. That was and remains the main force behind the big US trade deficit and not the high value of dollar. The US is faced with a dilemma: either it must give up the newly built international trading regimes or raise protection walls. Both choices have serious consequences.

Tragically, the situation of internal de-industrialization in the ADCs has become a policy instrument for putting pressures on the LDCs to open their markets and accept their own de-industrialization or face deceleration of capital and technology transfer. No effort is spared to put pressure on LDCs to yield on intellectual property rights. The aim is to destroy the R&D base of the LDCs; it is another version of Darwinism. Darwinism is not a single general linear theory. It is very complex and does not lend itself to prediction. The demand for the opening of the LDC markets is to reduce their leverage further. Labour cost differentials, which once formed the core of international trade theory, are no longer considered relevant. The advantages are nullified by tariff barriers or by denying to LDCs capacities to develop their potentials.

The structural changes that are forcing themselves on the ADCs, leaving out the LDCs, are breaking even old tenacious bonds. The ADCs, facing structural unemployment, partly created by economic reasons and partly by political objectives, are passing on the burden to the LDCs through rapid development of high capital and technology-intensive sectors and industries that are replacing older industries using ADC materials. ADC economies are getting integrated with similar other economies but moving away from all the LDCs, even from those who had managed to make some progress. Industries run with robots and with pre-programmed microchip brains that can do complex routine work requiring superhuman strength have no use for the LDCs except as markets which also do not exist in large measure. It is expected that by the end of this century the ADCs will have no more than 15 per cent of their population engaged in manufactures. This structural change will make trade between ADCs and LDCs decline and not increase any further.

The ADCs are insisting on including services in the new round of GATT discussions. They insist on including services as their mutual economic relations will depend upon how they cooperate over services. But for the LDCs it will mean the end of the world. Their elites will enjoy the services which will be replaced by high-grade services from the ADCs. The inclusion of service sectors in GATT means that the entire comparative advantage will shift to those who can effectively utilize information technology. At present 95 per cent of this technology is with the ADCs. Other factor endowments will become less significant as will the low cost of labour. We already know the fate of UNESCO's attempts to have a new information and communication order. Now the division will be complete, so will be the global economic and technological fracturing.

New technologies are pressing upon the ADCs, particularly the EEC, to get integrated as soon as they can. Technological competitiveness is pushing the ADCs to cooperate fast even if it means partial surrender of their sovereignties. The multinationals are also pushing their business in the same direction. In a couple of decades we will have the USA, USSR, China and Japan as a club of giant nations with military and non-military technological monopolies.

One does not know what will happen to the middle income group nations but the chances are that most will slip down the ladder. The LDCs in general will be out of the technological world.

The stalking of the global negotiations on the New International Economic Order has further exposed the irrelevance of interdependence as a positive arrangement between nations. Not only are the first and second world nations divided among themselves on the question of global negotiations, together they have almost put the third world on notice that for quite some time to come there will be no negotiations and no further transfer of resources, finance and technology except whatever is available in the market. If this is the state of affairs and the LDCs are obliged to go to the market and are denied all concessional rates or technological transfers, then one should know the consequences. We are also told that if only the developed countries were to reduce their production margins, tariff rates and other protectionist measures, the developing countries will have no problems. But this is also a marginal issue. How much of trade can really help the developing countries to solve their problems of development, poverty and unemployment removal is not clear. But one thing is certain: if some new growth may take place with trade expansion, there is no certainty that poverty and the unemployment position will improve. If, therefore, the NIEO is to be strengthened through more trade and decline in protectionism, it may be self-defeating.

Another common feature of the present international debate is the holding of regular international economic and monetary conferences. These conferences merely repeat old clichés about issues that have been debated at the Economic Committee of the UN, the UNCTAD, the FAO and the UNIDO. The UN agencies have produced no results; they simply legitimize the prevailing order or disorder. The same people meet again and again and produce the same results. If interdependence means more international debates, we cannot be very optimistic about the outcome of such hollow debates.

An important test of interdependence is how far the ADCs are going to allow international migration from the LDCs. It is dangerous to drain away highly skilled people from the developing LDCs while keeping unskilled people back. Since skills play a crucial role in economic development, the gap between the ADCs and LDCs will increase if the present pattern of migration continues. Thus, so-called interdependence can only produce a negative impact on growth. This may not be the propitious time to talk about the so-called large-scale transfer of labour, a time when there is massive unemployment also within the ADCs. But this is not true of every place. Vast areas of Canada, Australia, the Soviet Union and even the United States which remain undeveloped can absorb large amounts of surplus labour from the South. Greater labour mobility is the crucial test of true interdependence.

It is dangerous to put the entire blame for the emerging dependency on the machinations and policies of the ADCs. An even a greater responsibility rests on the modes of power and functioning of the leaders and institutions in the developing countries. The integration of the ruling elites of the developing world with those of the developed world has almost become complete, no matter what their foreign policies and ideological pretensions. The widening gap between the rich and the poor in the developing countries can be maintained only by the prevailing pattern of international integration. It is no accident that the development models of third world countries assume a much larger input from foreign finance, foreign technology and foreign trade. The dependency syndrome has been created not only by unequal exchanges between nations but also by developments within nations.

It is also no accident that most of the developing countries are being ruled either by military dictatorships or by other authoritarian regimes through which they oppress and exploit their own people. The dependency theorists are right in saying that the economies of the periphery 'are without any internal dynamics of their own'. This is not wholly true, though internal dynamics is very much there. The dynamics is of internal repression, exploitation, widening of disparities, internal income transfers, etc. The internal unequal exchange is not a pure reflection of the external unequal exchange. The gap between the differences in productivity and differences in wages is as much internal as external.

There is thus a double polarization—polarization between the rich and the poor nations and polarization within the poor nations. The second polarization is sustained by the first. There is an internal structural fragmentation within the developing countries which gets easily linked with the external polarization, widening the gap at all levels. International trade and domestic dualities get easily enmeshed. For instance, the so-called modern sectors in the developing countries may be as modern as those in the developed countries but they do not possess technological strength to sustain themselves. This is the process by which dependency and interdependence get integrated. But the same polarization now is taking the form of rupture or Darwinism.

It is from the premises of interdependence that the demand for a New International Economic Order arises. The debate, unlike the debate on disarmament, has proceeded along impossible lines. The participants have been insincere, selfish and have always tried to use the negotiations for their own advantage. Above all, the powerful nations have made assumptions and laid claims which the poor nations could never accept and if some of them did accept, they have done no more than pay lip-service to such claims and assumptions. The whole debate about the NIEO has been phoney. Indeed there seems to be a high correlation between the high-pitch debate and the widening disparities between the rich and the poor classes, between the two sets of nations, as well as within the poorer nations themselves.

Leaving out the fantacies indulged in by Kahn, Weiner and others, there have been four respectable models that were proposed and which flopped even within the limits of their own conceptual framework and more so when put into operation. The first most talked about was the Pretisch or UNCTAD model of the first decade of development. That was for the sixties. For the subsequent decade and years, three models were put by (i) the Pearson Commission of which Lester Pearson, former Canadian Prime Minister was the Chairman, (ii) a group of experts working under Sir Robert Jackson, which was set up by the UNDP, (iii) the Developing Planning Committee of the UN that advises the Secretary General.

All the four models are variations of the same theories which include (i) high growth rates in all nations, individually as well as when grouped together; (ii) transfer of resources for accelerating development in poor nations; (iii) liberalization of trade with protection rights guaranteed only to developing nations on an infant industry basis; (iv) new restructuring of share of manufacturing between developed and developing nations if only as an adjunct of the liberal trading system and to end protectionism everywhere in the long run.

Chronologically the real debate about the NIEO took nearly 25 years after the end of World War II. It began with UNCTAD Ist (1969) and the GSP (1971), followed by the formation of G-77. Till that time the emphasis was on commodity price stabilization. The

Lima Conference of 1975 extended the scope of the debate by including (i) integrated prrogramme of commodities; (ii) creation of a common fund and the demand for zero per cent of GDP of the developed world to be transferred to the developing nations. The proposals of the Lima Conference are practically dead. Subsequent attempts made at every international monetary conference, both on exchange rates and strengthening the international financial institutions, did not evoke a positive response from the ADCs.

The rationale of the NIEO has faced opposing perspectives. The poor nations which have emerged as politically independent from long periods of colonialism recently feared that the prevailing economic, trade and finance arrangements in a world which was dominated by the old and new imperial powers, would work to their disadvantage and might even abridge their political independence. This fear was not unfounded. Most surprisingly, what has happened is that the ruling classes of the poor nations, while expressing these fears and hoping for a better alternative, ultimately became willing junior partners in the continuation of the prevailing order. This is the centre, the core of relations of interdependence.

The division of the world on political-military-strategic lines and the formation of military blocs created a cold war climate in which no new world order was feasible. Attempts were made by both the old imperial powers and the new rising imperial states to use the cold war for fostering military dependence on the former colonies in the name of security. This had serious economic implications. The formation of military blocs was bound to lead to economic relations tied down to security priorities. The demand for an NIEO was made as an economic counterforce against military blocs. Once again the outcome was quite contrary to the expectations. The developing nations, whether they remained part of a military bloc or outside it, suffered almost equally in the economic sense. In fact, those nations which faithfully borrowed the ideology of the imperial powers did somewhat better. There was uneven development in respect of every combination.

It was accepted by everybody, including Marxists and the international institutions, that the prevailing order that emerged from World War II was highly deterimental to the interests of the poorer nations irrespective of security or other considerations. The period of colonial exploitation left the new independent nations with completely tattered economies. They were extremely short of resources, technical manpower and even consumer goods. There was no money even for food. These considerations which made the poorer nations subject to the onslaught of various bloc formations, group formations, obliged them to press their claims for an NIEO.

The components of the restructuring of the prevailing order were few but vital. The LDCs demanded (i) a remunerative price for their commodities and more favourable commodity terms of trade; (ii) bilateral and multilateral transfer of capital and other resources; (iii) creation of international funds and other liquidity assets for price support and other mechanisms needed for stabilization of relations; (iv) sharing of technological progress, etc. Other demands were of minor significance. The entire debate about the NIEO has revolved around these four components and on each of these issues, the outcome has been contrary to the interests of the LDCs. In this, the ADCs and the ruling classes of the developing nations as well as international agencies, especially the UN, have been co-conspirators.

The developing nations tried to form themselves into loose globally viewed blocs rather than structure their groups on some solid basis. For instance, the so-called group of nations called G-77, the main body clamouring for the NIEO, has been more of a debating forum notwithstanding the fact that its membership today stands at 125. They are dubbed as so many zeros. The body is politically divided and the economic interests of one group are inconsistent with other groups. Some members are mere puppets in the hands of one or the other nation of the first or the second developed group. And above all, almost all the wars going on in the world are confined to members of this group. Their lack of coherence, unity and agreement on perspective have been exploited by the developed world to the maximum. In fact the largest and yet the most ineffective group which is clamouring for NIEO is the G-77. The ADCs have always treated this group with contempt.

The NAM group of nations and the G-77 overlap. The former has 102 members and the latter 125. From both forums they talk about NIEO. G-77 is supposed to confine itself to economic matters and the NAM to whatever it considers important. Since each group of nations has different economic priorities, for dovetailing economic and non-economic issues in order to make maximum impact on the developed world required a different arrangement. In fact the 125 developing nations should have grouped themselves on a regional or functional basis rather than getting lumped together and often fighting among themselves. Consequently, there has been total failure of any serious South-South cooperation in the formation of solid blocs within the developing nations for pressing on towards an NIEO.

The biggest failure of the NIEO has been the total absence of the creation of any South-South cooperation. While something by way of dialogue has been gone through in every other respect of the NIEO, there has been no movement at all on South-South cooperation. It seems that the developing nations suspect one another more than they suspect their old or new imperial powers. India and Pakistan, Egypt and Libya, Iraq and Iran, Uganda and Tanzania, etc., are examples of bilateral relations among developing nations causing serious frictions within the G-77 at political levels. Without South-South interdependence how can there be any North-South interdependence?

Some of the UN agencies like UNCTAD, GATT, UNIDO and FAO make the claim that they have been responsible for both maintaining the tempo of the debate on NIEO as well as helping initiate some action on the aforementioned components of the NIEO. Looking back one can see the zero effect of the kind of noises made at these forums in defence of the interests of the developing nations. No wonder, ultimately, UN international bureaucracy ended up defending its own interests against everybody else. These agencies could not criticize the exploitation of the masses by the ruling elites of the developing natioons. They refused to make proposals beyond what the international controllers of finance and capital permitted. They tried to give preference to one or the other group of nations. If the debate about the NIEO is dead, it is partly because of the failure of the international bureaucracy. Like the debate on disarmament, the debate on NIEO has also moved out of the UN. We had seen the spectacle of the Brandt Commission producing no results.

At best, the NIEO is a distant vision; at worst it is a populist deception. Dissatisfaction expressed about the established economic positions and relations is a mould 'of mutually excluding ideas about these matters, and a solution which one considers to go too far, sacrificing the major achievements of one hundred years of economic development, is criticized by other as merely scratching the surface without any potential to solve the underlying problems.' This is a terribly pessimistic view, a view 'which seems justified, as only minor adjustment can be expected from negotiations, levelling out smaller menaces to economics of negotiating partners .[10]

The central problem is that there is no consensus on economic basis of relations between (i) small and big nations; (ii) between small and medium nations; (iii) between developed and poor nations in terms of technology and so on. Each is in a different phase. In the absence of a theory of economic independence, there can be no serious theory of interdependence. The essential requirements for functional interdependence have not been worked out, even if it is believed that it is neither possible nor necessary to have a theory of economic independence. The following imperatives are too obvious to ignore. Firstly, one should bring out in quantitative terms the nature of interdependence of the various entities involved in the process. Secondly, the extent of sharing of benefits and costs should be brought out clearly in a dynamic setting so that the nature of conflicts of interests could be identified. Thirdly, one should work out alternative schemes of trade-offs and side payments which convert the situation of conflict into one of complementarity. Finally, the various strategies and policies   required to nourish, sustain and develop the environment of   complementarity should be identified and widely publicized.

Interdependence in reality has meant that the LDCs in economic difficulties and in need of external economic assistance are pressed on by the west, World Bank and IMF to adopt economic policies that are unacceptable to the donees in return for aid. More often than not, these policies, reluctantly accepted by the recipient nations, end up in deepening their crisis and threatening the survival of their governments. Generally, the policies that are pushed down the throat of the fragile economies are a set of austere measures. That is not all. To those policies are added the demands for a drastic shifts towards the private sector. Although no one poor nation can claim that its public sector functions efficiently or produces economic surpluses even at half the market rate of interest, let alone the average profit rate, the private sector performs only a little better and that, by exploiting the public sector. How much private is private is enigmatic. Probably the most brutal way poor nations are blackmailed is the ADC threat to withhold aid if policies recommended are not accepted. This often leads to unrest, street demonstrations and even the breakdown of administration and even the

[10] Soogfreed Pauswang, 'A New International Economic Order' in R.P. Misra and Nguya Tri Dung (eds), *Third World Peasantry*, Sterling, New Delhi, 1986, pp. 8-9.

fall of governments.

As discussed earlier, the current debate about the NIEO revolves around (i) dependency and (ii) interdependence. There is no essential difference between the two. The interdependence of developed and developing nations, as it has been shaped over the last four decades, has been having a relation of dependency and loss of autonomy of the developing nations in respect of their economic policies. It has also been shown that the various demands which the developing countries themselves have made in the name of NIEO have been so structured that they have made them more dependent. For instance, the demand for transfer of capital has made the developing world groan under the international debt problem. It has also been shown that if all the demands of the developing countries were met through the NIEO, the result would be the same—the creation of a dependency syndrome. However, the dead silence that has fallen on the NIEO dabate is an expression of the fact that the situation has moved beyond the pale of dependence or interdependence. No one is listening and no one wants to listen. If the so-called international community has gone deaf, the situation is alarmingly Darwinist.

Finally, the test of theory or hypothesis lies not only in its explanatory power of past events, but also in its current operations. In the May 1990 meeting of the IMF, the US proved her aggressive Darwinism which shocked most members; the US, while agreeing to doubling the IMF quota, made it conditional upon throwing out the eleven poorest nations from IMF membership. The US relented somewhat but did not give up the principle of linking the IMF quota increase with the provision of punishing its erring members. It is an irony that LDC Finance Ministers who were addressing the ministerial-level development committee of IMF, World Bank, repeated the old cliches, calling upon ADCs to remove poverty by the year 2000.

The Report of the South Commission entitled 'Challenge of the South' is an exhaustive survey of the problems of development, political integration and lifestyles in the LDCs and the South. It is probably the best report ever prepared within the context of the present international order. Its fault lies in the fact that basically, it is based on the principles of interdependence and therefore suffers from all the inadmissible asumptions, constraints and platitudes which characterize the model of interdependence. The report has dealt adequately with the problems both of the North-South relations and South-South cooperation but the entire exercise has been done on the assumption that it is possible to improve the situation in the South within the present global order. The report has been candid enough to point out the difficulties and hurdles in the way of both types of cooperation. Yet the report is very optimistic, as it could not be otherwise. Probably for the first time the report has talked about developing the *South consciousness*. There is no such consciousness at present nor is there much scope for its emergence in the near future. It is so because it has missed answers to three very important questions: (i) the dependence of the ruling elites of the South and the North and their internal resistance to mobilisation of the South; (ii) the Darwinist trends that flow from the external policies of the North or the ADCs; and (iii) the massive poverty of the masses which is acting as a barrier against any movement for social transformation. In reality the South Commission's Report is an extended version of the Brandt Commission Report. Therefore, it is unlikely to produce any serious changes in the prevailing order. Like its predecessors, it remains the hope and the despair of the South.

TOWARDS AN ALTERNATIVE
PARADIGM – I

The Gandhian Response

Whether the aforementioned disorder is *sui generis* or a symptom or manifestation of some other deeper disorder can be debated and there would be different views and interpretations. But few can deny that these are manifest disorders that humanity faces. Paradoxically, it is the response in terms of solutions over which there are sharp disagreements. Whereas there is almost a consensus on the need for disarmament, reduction of debt, elimination of poverty, defence of human rights, protection of environments, etc., the consensus is more philosophical than practical. Therefore, at a superficial level, it might seem that the analysis of the disordered situation and the solution thereof are matters of general agreement, but it is inertia, lack of general agreement on policies, lack of political will, vested interests, etc., that are standing in the way of a resolution of the crisis.

This is only partly so. Indeed, impediments are a crisis within a crisis. The global power system and its constitutions, including the ruling elites of the LDCs, but not the people of the South, seem to contribute to this consensus. The debates in the UN and its specialised agencies, which are all constituted by government representatives, have proved not only the futility of this organisation but also of the consensus arrived there. Billions of words have been written, thousands of conferences have been held, hundreds and thousands of intellectuals have participated simply to discover the lowest common denominator. Mountains seem to have been moved to produce a mouse.

As mentioned in the earlier chapters, it is important to make a distinction between the people or the nation on the one hand and the state or government and the power elite on the other. It is the power elite and not the people who are responsible for war and peace. Gandhi had said, 'I had used the expression *warring nations*, not the peoples of Europe. I have distinguished between the nation and its leaders.'[1] It is important to define the respective roles of the state, the nation, the elite or leaders and the people.

A Gandhian response to the global disorder would not merely hit the disorder in the face but hit the global power system in the belly. The whole order is structured in a way that it cannot but produce crises beyond solution. Every solution suggested or applied so far has perpetuated the existing system or applied so far has perpetuated the existing system with some protests and with crumbs from the high table for the protestors.

What really are the Gandhian reflections on the contemporary global disorder? First, it is the crisis or tyranny of concepts about the reality. For instance, to say that there is such a thing as an international community or one world or concern for the poor, etc., is a conceptual deception. In terms of economics, it is not one world but many worlds, each drifting away from the other and yet linked in a way in which unity of thought and action on the basis of universal justice cannot be established. Indeed, it is a fractured world with each fraction trying to become more autonomous and working in conflict with the other.

It has been shown that no matter what classification of the global system is used, it is quite obvious that the ADCs are getting more and more integrated into a single economic system, by the design, the dialectics and the dynamics of their systems. The members of the ADCs invest more in each other's countries, trade mostly within one another, share each other's prosperity, create new monopolies and oligopolies, all within a competitive situation. The communist world, despite all hopes and fears, is now disintegrating. Schemes, plans, arrangements are being made all the time to integrate it into one ADC economy. In this manner they hope to improve their share in global trade, sometimes at the cost of the LDCs.

To bring back the world into unity, several conditions must be satisfied, the most important being the replacement of the nation-state system. We are living in a world of nation-states that both constitute the global system and also fracture the international

[1] *Harijan*, 29 Sept. 1940

community. There are micro states, middle powers, super powers, giant nations, etc. The world cannot remain in peace and stability so long as the inequalities caused by the size differences among nations permit a few to dominate many others persist. It is proved beyond doubt that social systems make little difference. The Soviet Union, the United States, Western Europe, the giant nations or coalitions in size and resources, have emerged as super powers as well as imperial systems. There might be others like Japan in the queue. The state as the very unit level of the global system is detrimental to the integrity and unity of humanity. The concept of interdependence has been exposed as a legitimiser of the prevailing system. Theories and relations that are based on absolute sovereignty and relations between sovereign nations can only produce interdependence that sanctifies domination of one set of nations over others. International relations are there but concepts explaining them are absolute myths. Under the prevailing system, either there will be no peace to stability or if there is, it is the peace and stability of the grave or of a new oligopolistic imperial system of exploitation generating Darwinism in the end.

It must be stressed here that the Gandhian approach is the dynamics and dialectics of a relation between the ideas and their feasibility, both being present in equal measure. That is why Gandhi called himself a *practical idealist*. There are several Gandhian principles and approaches for restructuring the global system in the foreseeable future. These principles are idealistic as well as very practical.

The first is world federation as stated in a resolution drafted by Gandhi himself and passed by the AICC in 1942. The Quit India Movement Resolution was remarkable in many ways. It sought India's freedom not as a culmination of a nationalist exclusiveness but as part of a world federation of free nations. In fact, the Committee was quite categorical.

> While the AICC must primarily be concerned with the independence and defence of India in this hour of danger, the Committee is of the opinion that the future peace, security and ordered progress of the world demand a world federation of free nations, and on no other basis can the problems of the modern world would be solved. Such a World Federation would ensure the freedom of its constituent nations, the prevention of aggression and exploitation by one nation over

another, the protection of national minorities, the advance-
ment on all backward areas and peoples, and the pooling of
the world's resources for the common good of all. On the establishment of such a World Federation, disarmament would
be practicable in all countries, national armies, navies and air
forces would no longer be necessary, and a World/Federal
Defence Force would keep the world peace and prevent aggression.

An independent India would gladly join such a World Federation and cooperate on an equal basis with other nations in
the solution of international problems.

There was a great hope that after an initial period of adjustment
UN would slowly move towards some kind of a loose federation.
This has not happened. Instead all the divisions of the world are
reflected in UN under a thin veneer of cooperation and the so-called
convergence of national interests. The biggest failure of the UN has
been in the area of ensuring security of nations. Besides there are
aggressive economic nationalism, regional groupings and the desire
to exploit rather than cooperate. This brings me to the second
Gandhian response which requires people as much as nations to be
the actors on the global stage, particularly the UN.

Problems such as environmental pollution, nuclear threats,
exploitation of the seas and space, etc., which by their national
boundaries must be brought under a system of pooled sovereignties, in a limited way to begin with and to be enlarged later. The
suggested subjects are crises issues that need such pooling. To be
practical, a struggle for the next half century will not be for the
setting up of a world government but for focussing on the areas
where sovereignties can be abridged and pooled. Those nations
which sit on vast natural resources will not agree to it. The developing countries have done themselves no good by trying to be
jealous of their limited resources, thus giving a handle to the rich
nations to sit on their own resources. In the struggle for economic
nationalism, the strong will not only stage a march over the weak,
but also exploit them. Some natural resources have to be declared
as the property of the global community over which national
sovereignty must not be exercises. The point I am making is that a
right beginning made over the pooling of national sovereignties
would be the first step towards a world government which may
come after many decades or even a century.

A more detailed, careful analysis and response are needed for ending the arms race, transferring weapons to LDCs, reducing defence budgets, declining technologies from their use in improving the quality of weapon systems and above all the general militarisation of societies, particularly by the LDC dictators and through inter-state disputes. The global system completely ignores the security of small nations, so much so that the preoccupation with security leads to bondage. The current debate on disarmament and methods to reduce the arms race leaves out the LDCs or makes them take up the lag.

One might ask the questions as to why the USSR and the USA are negotiating to eliminate weapons of mass destruction. The reason is simple: these armaments have reached a critical point where they have become inconsistent with the economic growth of the respective economies. Besides, the same weapons are also more an instrument of nuclear blackmail. They are not reducing their weapons because they have become benign, but for economic reasons.

A Gandhian response to the present situation would demand something which produces more effective as well as realistic results. It should give equal priority to disarmament, reduction of defence expenditure, elimination of military-industrial complexes, reduction in the sale of arms, demilitarisation of societies and the use of funds saved from defence for development and social justice programmes. Development strategy for a largely disarmed world is quite different from that which is armed heavily.

Global security and trading systems are inseprable. Given the complexity of arms control negotiations, the following steps will have to be taken. First, agreements arrived at for the reduction of missiles and weapons must be accompanied by some reduction in the defence budgets, without which, given the tremendous opportunities created by new technologies, the super powers will be producing some other weapons of mass destruction. There is only one way to slow down the race towards new kinds of weaponry, namely, to cut down defence budgets. As a first step, there must be a total freeze on the existing budgets for the next two or three years. Next, there should be at least one per cent reduction in the defence budget every year for the next ten years. Second, the principles of freeze or reduction of defence budgets will have to be accepted by all nations. Some of the poor nations are spending on defence a larger percentage of their GDP than the developed countries. Third, although a general reduction in defence budgets of all countries would itself constrain international trading in arms, special measures on the part of the big powers would be required to reduce the flow of arms from one country to another. Fourth, since nearly two-thirds of scientific and technical manpower in the ADCs are employed in war industries, a limit has to be placed on this proportion immediately. Without these changes being accepted, the global economy will always remain in disorder and encourage Darwinism.

The reduction in arms, defence budgets and in the flow of arms would save a great deal of money. This money will have to be utilized in a way that benefits the victims of the arms race. A substantial part of the money, saved from the elimination of weapons and the reduction of defence budgets should be put in a common global pool for investment in the poor nations. Otherwise the disarmament exercise will create no confidence in the majority of the people of the world. Public opinion and the vested interest in the developed countries would resist this kind of transfer, but without which the commitment to peace would be nil. For that and other reasons not a penny from this pool should go to the governments of the third world countries. It is a common experience that a large part of the aid given to the third world countries goes into the pockets of the corrupt ruling elites. Only a small percentage of the aid goes to the deserving.

Within all defence parameters, for more than two decades, literally thousands of scholars and hundreds of institutions have been involved in making noises about a new economic order. Yet there is not even a beginning, not even a consensus on some fundamental principles of the new order, let alone any one seriously going about reconstructing it. There is no point in discussing here an abstract concept that has already been discussed many times over.

However, there are four propositions which arise from the Gandhian philosophy, and these are of a practical nature. If genuine disarmament takes place and corresponding financial resources are released, without doubt a part of these resources should be earmarked for the development of the poor nations. So far as the poor nations are concerned they do not gain anything whether there are more or less nuclear weapons with the super powers. In fact, there is a danger that nuclear disarmament might generate new pressures for the sale of conventional arms to the third world countries. It has already been pointed out earlier that disarmament must be accompanied by a reduction in defence budgets and the money thus saved should be used for development.

Second, the money allocated for development should be put in a common global pool that would be administered by a new international agency, that is not controlled by governments or their representatives. It would certainly not be controlled by any present UN agency. Ultimately all aid has been, one way or another, an instrument of economic exploitation, whether bilateral or multilateral if the negotiating parties are governments.

Third, so far, most of the aid given to the poor countries has been pocketed by their rulers and the middle classes. Therefore, the money put in the common pool will also have to be administered by non-governmental agencies within a nation so that the truly poor and not their masters benefit. A system will have to be evolved which satisfies two conditions: (a) aid would go for development aimed at poverty elimination, and (b) the beneficiaries will themselves administer the aid. Thus the idea of a global economic fund administered by non-governmental agencies at both ends will have to be accepted as a basic principle of the new integration economic order. One of the reasons why the new order has not come about is that the ruling elites of the third world have become subservient developed countries. That is also why there is no credibility for their demand for a new international economic order. The principle of abridged sovereignties will have to be tested in respect of the use of aid. Both the donor and the donee governments will have to give up part of their rights to decide.

Fourth, one of the fundamental Gandhian principles is that trade is not to be expanded for its own sake. A large quantum of trade between nations today does not generate use values. It is only designed to cater to artificially created demands. If the present trends are allowed to continue, sooner or later there would be a serious economic crisis from which the poor countries will suffer even more. No one has seriously discussed Gandhian trade principles and it is high time that poor nations cease to be victims of pressures from international trade regimes and international trading agencies. Elsewhere I have attempted a first exercise in delineating Gandhi's theories of international trade.[2]

There are two Gandhian principles of trade. First, there should

[2] J.D. Sethi, 'Gandhian Theory and Philosophy of International Trade', *Gandhi Marg*, Oct.-Dec., 1989.

be no or only limited trade in those goods which specifically meet the basic needs of the people, unless those goods cannot be locally produced. Certainly the theory of comparative cost will not apply in respect of basic needs. Second, there will be no trade in what might be called inessentials. The inessentials are those for which the comparative advantage cannot be proved at all on non-economic grounds, and even if there is such an advantage on economic grounds, there will still be no trade if it flows from the falsification of wants. Within the limits of these two constraints, new trading principles have to be defined and also the self-reliance redefined.

Since in many respects technologies are neutral between weapons and civilian production, as well as between one kind of civilian production and another, there has also to be a pool of technologies which would help produce at the lowest cost goods needed to satisfy the basic needs of the people but without damaging environment. If there is no check on the direction of technological improvements, the whole exercise of arms control might be defeated. The number of weapons might be refaced but their deadly quality and precision might improve and thus create more uncertainty. Besides, without a proper control and distribution of technologies and technologists, the inequalities of the global order will accentuate. Above all, without breaking the nexus between the ruling elites of the developed world and the developed countries there would never be genuine peace.

The prevailing global order, or any of the suggested alternatives, whether coming from ADCs or LDCs, point towards some marginal changes and alleviation measures. Exploitation, poverty, and alienation, which are the central problems of humanity, their solution demands a complete global re-ordering, but this is not accepted. There are about one billion people who are destitutes. There are another one billion who along with the first mentioned one billion constitute those whom the World Bank would characterise as living below the poverty line. In terms of quality of life, out of the world population of five billion, at least two-thirds live under one or the other kind of economic and social deprivation. It is not surprising that at least two-thirds of the people of the world are those who are denied elementary political rights.

According to Gandhian philosophy, poverty and denial of freedom are two sides of the same problem and, therefore, cannot be tackled separately, at least as far as the LDCs are concerned. This is clear to some extent from the examples of the West European,

American and Japanese democracies, even though there is a high degree of inequality in their respective systems. The past trend of interdependent exploitation of the LDCs by the ADCs has been weakened giving place to Darwinism, because the trend of economic development of the ADCs is to get more and more integrated among themselves and marginalise the rest of the world. That is why, in a Gandhian framework, increasing economic integration between ADCs and LDCs would mean further exploitation and perpetuation of poverty. Darwinism is more dangerous and immoral than straight imperialism or dependency.

A Gandhian response to the problems of international economic order would not be for larger trade or aid and increasing transfer of technology. These solutions would be only exceptions to the general rule of self-reliance which would comprise of two concepts: Swaraj (self-rule) and Swadeshi (self-reliance). Swaraj is a much more comprehensive concept than mere political independence. In fact, judging by the Gandhian concept of Swaraj, most of the LDCs are even more enslaved than they were under direct colonial rule. Now they are under double exploitation of the old colonial rulers and their junior partners at home. The linkage between the old imperial powers and the newly independent countries is between two ruling classes which result in double exploitation, more poverty and a greater loss of freedom. Swaraj is not mere democracy but much more. We shall examine the options of the LDCs in the light of the aforementioned possible Gandhian responses.

Lest we should misunderstand Gandhi's concept of Swaraj or Swadeshi or self-reliance or nationalism, let me give his views which speak for themselves.

> We want freedom for our country but not at the expense or exploitation of others, not so as to degrade other countries. I do not want the freedom of India, if it means the extinction of England or disappearance of Englishmen. I want the freedom of my country so that other countries may learn something from my free country, so that the resources of my country might be utilised for the benefit of mankind. Just as the cult of patriotism teaches us today that the individual has to die for the family, the family has to die for the village, the village for the district, the district for the province, the province for the country, even so, a country has to be free in order that it may

die, if necessary, for the benefit of the world. My love, therefore, of nationalism, or my idea of nationalism, is that my
country may become free, so that if need be the whole country
may die so that the human race may live.[3]

No international system can ever be just and peaceful if it is
based on exploitation. The entire modern theory of international
trade is a theory of exploitation. That is why Gandhi said that the
'Economics that permit one country to prey upon another are
immoral.'[4] The prevailing paradigm of international economic relations is highly immoral and leading to International Economic
Darwinism.

[3] N.K. Bose, *Selections from Gandhi*, Navajivan Press, Ahmedabad, 1948, p. 43.
[4] Quoted by B.N. Ganguli, *Gandhi's Social Philosophy*, Vikas, Delhi, 1973, p. 64.

TOWARDS AN ALTERNATIVE
PARADIGM – II

Detach and Attach

If the prevailing situation and its projections of the international economic situation do conform to what has been stated earlier then the task before the LDCs to regenerate their economies as a part of the prevailing international system and paradigm is hopeless. The structures and compulsions of the present order are increasingly integrating developed countries, both socialist and capitalist, in respect of trade, security and culture. All the recent statements made by Gorbachev and China's open door policy to the west despite domestic repression, fully endorse these trends.

Since all the LDCs are of different sizes, are not at the same level of development, have wide differences in resource endowment, located in different strategic positions, and, above all, are led by elites of varying quality and commitment, there can be no single solution for them to fight International Darwinism. A variety of strategies will have to be developed.

However, even if such strategies were available, the integration of the ruling elites of the LDCs with those of the ADCs, while the masses are being marginalized by both, will militate against the adoption of such strategies. International corruption has become the most important instrument in the hands of those who control the global system, purchase the ruling elites of the LDCs and integrate them with those of the ADCs. At present there is no mechanism outside the governmental organization by which desired changes can be effected.

All efforts to initiate a dialogue on the New International Economic Order (NIEO) have totally failed. This is not because different nations or groups of nations have different perceptions of the new order, but because the existing order eminently suits most of the ADCs. The matter does not end here. This order also suits the ruling elites of most of the LDCs, notwithstanding the noises they make in favour of change. More significantly the objectives set for an NIEO and the terms of the debate do not make the debate feasible. The LDCs are caught in a cleft stick. Their leaders shout about the NIEO but are unprepared to accept changes in the rules of the game from which they benefit enormously as a class.

Marxists had claimed once that socialist revolution could change the situation. Unfortunately, three recent developments have reduced the relevance of Marxism. First, the Marxist economic paradigm is now recognized as being much the same as the non-Marxist ones. Both are oriented towards growth, capital accumulation and capital-labour substitution, economic rationality without morality, each having its own structure of power or class inequalities. Economists like Holbrenner, scientists like Kuhn, and philosophers like Habermas have convincingly proved that modern political economy, starting with Adam Smith, had been fashioned on a single paradigm, be it socialist, capitalist or any other. That is why neither interdependence nor dependency can provide a satisfactory solution to global crises. Second, the distribution of political and military power and its concentration in the hands of nation-states have made it difficult, if not impossible to export or produce indigenous Marxist revolution anywhere. In fact, in view of the great inequalities of power there is always a danger of the revolutionary spirit and fervour degenerating into terrorism. Third, with both the Soviet Union and China opting for market economy principles, the international movement for revolution has been eroded. Therefore, we have to go beyond capitalist and Marxist and other prevailing paradigms or theories.

Given the present grim situation and a continuous closing of options, the main thrust of the LDCs has to be a search for an alternative paradigm to the prevailing dominant ADCs' paradigm which, notwithstanding its external contradiction of opposing social systems, is pushing the LDCs towards rupture. To me the only alternative is the Gandhian paradigm. However, in view of its neglect at home, general intellectual scepticism, and absence of theoretical rigour and holistic approach, an elaborate model cannot be presented here for reasons of space. I have attempted to structure this paradigm in a book from which this paper has been culled out.

Space does not permit me also to present all its assumptions, concepts, actions, etc. It would be unfair to Gandhi and the readers to present a vague, perfunctory model. The best I can do is to infer from it the future course of action for LDCs based on some firmly held Gandhian propositions and go through the excruciating exercise of providing an answer to Darwinism in terms of the idioms and concepts of the prevailing paradigm.

No matter how the economic stream is arranged the paradigm would be of a moral political economy, the emphasis being equally on moral and political as on economic. At least one economist of repute, A.K. Sen, has moved in that direction. Five Gandhian propositions are mentioned below without elaboration or discussion.

First, so long as the world is dominated by what Gandhi called 'gangster nations', there can neither be world peace nor a just world order. One of the important determinants is the size of the nations, for generally, large-size nations have critical control over global resources. Their size makes them potential gangsters.

Second, the competition between nation-states under the conditions of the first proposition must inevitably lead to pluralistic imperialism and ultimately to imperialism, or its alternative, Darwinism. Unless the nation-states, step by step, yield sovereignty to form a world government, the LDCs will always remain second-rate citizens within the so-called international community. The UN system which was expected ultimately to create a world government has further entrenched the division of the globe into nation-states.

Third, international trade and foreign investments must be the outcome of domestic development strategies rather than be its determinants. No development strategy would be acceptable unless full employment and dignity of labour are ensured. Technology choices should be such as do not displace labour.

Fourth, trade between nations will not be conducted on the principle of comparative advantage or any other mainstream theory. There could be minimum or no trade at two ends of the trade spectrum, i.e., trade of goods of basic needs and of those which are non-essentials and instigated by consumerism, greed and other such human motivations. The theory that some trade is better than no trade has no place in the Gandhian paradigm.

Fifth, for both analytical and practical purposes we have to shift our conceptual perspective from the LDCs to the concept of the

South. It is a hopeless task to expect governments of the LDCs to mount a revolt against the present order. They are, in fact, a part of it. Sadly, the concept of South remains weak and vague. If South means the people of the LDCs as distinguished from their power elites, they may look for allies among the ADCs in the emerging forces such as the Greens, peace movements, radical intellectuals and even some governments of the ADCs which are small in size and have to struggle to fight the hegemonistic pressures of the big powers.

What can the LDCs do? First, without the LDCs pooling their sovereignties in respect of areas in which the ADCs' pressure is fierce, there can be no South-South cooperation. This cooperation is absolutely necessary to fight Darwinism. If the LDCs do not pay attention to this difficult issue, the ADCs would impose their own plans, priorities and instruments. One such instrument is the well-established system of multinationals, which is assuming new forms with more complex relations. It is recognized by some that:

> The concept of national boundaries requires re-examination. With the exchange of information becoming speedier and the interdependence of economic relations deepening, firms should not be bogged down by the conventional notion of state. They should simply identify the countries that ensure the best conditions for business activities and utilize the network for activities such as general production, marketing and R&D in a global perspective. This can be understood as a natural extension of the growth process of the firm. However in the sphere of politics, people are only allowed to exercise their rights to vote within the national boundaries, and the foreigners are excluded, *but in economies, while the political barriers created by national regulations exist, the concept of national boundaries exist in name.*[1]

In other words, the globalization activities which would become predominant will choose some nations and exclude others depending upon profitability, markets and management control.

Second, the LDCs will have to largely delink themselves from the ADCs in respect of their economic relations, particularly trade and aid relations. Total delinking is neither feasible nor desirable,

---

[1] T. Nakakita, *The Developing Economies*, Dec. 1988.

but the linkages must be subject to a well-chosen model. Besides, delinking will neither be total nor uniform for each country or for each relation. Paradoxically, trade which has assumed the highest priority has also become the main instrument of Darwinism. Therefore, the first priority will be to reduce the area of trade between the LDCs and the ADCs until such time that global inequalities are reduced.

J.M. Keynes, the father of a modern international economic order, had said long ago:

> I sympathize, therefore, with those who would minimize, rather than with those who would maximize, economic entanglement among nations. Ideas, knowledge, science, hospitality, travel—these are the things which should of their nature be international. But let goods be homespun whenever it is reasonable and conveniently possible, and above all, let finance be primarily national . . . .
> The decadent international but individualist capitalism in the hands of which we found ourselves after the war, is not a success. It is not intelligent, it is not beautiful, it is not just, it is not virtuous and it doesn't deliver the goods. In short, we dislike it, and we are beginning to despise it. . . . We do not wish, therefore, to be at the mercy of world forces working out, or trying to work out, some uniform equilibrium according to the ideal principles if they can be called such, of laissez-faire capitalism. We wish . . . to be our own masters, and to be as free as we can make ourselves from the interferences of the outside world.[2]

This Keynesian view has been indicated by new trends and developments. The whole basis of modern international relationship is based on the fact that world trade has grown faster than world output. This has been interpreted as the world becoming more interdependent. This is a half-truth, because the results produced are adverse to the LDCs which are under strong theoretical and economic pressures for the ultra-pro-trade-biased obiter dicta of the professional mainstream. Since this mainstream is now running against the interests of the LDCs, an alternative trading

    [2] Surendra J. Patel, *Economic Theory and New World Order*, Ashish, New Delhi, 1987, p. 602.

paradigm and regime are needed for the reasons given below.

The prevailing trading system and its theoretical foundations have reinforced the differential economic status of the ADCs and LDCs. There are many reasons for it, but as Kitimura has emphasized, the status assumptions of the trade theory, including fixity of production, technology and stocks of productive resources on the one hand and the economies of scale given to nation-states on the other, have delegitimized the theory. Kitimura further argued that 'in a changing world of capital accumulation and technological progress, free trade does not tend to maximize the welfare of the less developed countries in order to ensure their balance of trade'.[3]

Although the ADCs have achieved high wage rates in contrast to those in the LDCs, the ratio of productivity to wage rate is higher in the richer countries because of the control over technologies and natural resources, both of which give them a strong base for higher rates of productivity growth. Consequently, capital is attracted to the richer than to the poorer nations, increasing the technological gap and the international difference in wage levels. This means that both free and controlled trade are unlikely to increase the relative capital endowments of the LDCs.[4]

The economies of scale established in manufacturing in the ADCs and the absence of such economies in mining and agriculture in the LDCs continued to strengthen the competitive position of manufacturing in the ADCs. The gap has been widening and trade has become instrumental in widening the gap. The more the push towards trade, the larger becomes the gap.

Capital-intensive enclaved economy has been confined to manufacturing for specific classes. Even in respect of plantation and mining, the production of which is largely exported, there is marked capital intensity relative to the rest of the economy. The infrastructure development and imports required to maintain the export sector in plantation and mining have failed to produce backward linkages into input supplying industries or forward linkages into secondary industries.[5]

[3] K. Kitimura, 'Capital Accumulation and the Theory of International Trade', *Malayan Economic Review*, Vol. 3, No. 1, reprinted in I. Livingstone (ed.), *Economic Policy for Development*, Penguin, 1971, p. 81.

[4] Barrot Brown, *The Economics of Imperialism*, Penguin, 1974.

[5] G.L. Backford, *Persistent Poverty: Underdevelopment in Plantation Economies in the Third World*, Oxford University Press, 1972.

Transport handling, insurance charges and other services connected with trade almost entirely accrue to the ADCs. Countries
which own large merchant fleets or have developed sophisticated
insurance and banking services appropriate a large part of the
advantages derived from trade. Despite all the attempts by the
LDCs to develop these services the advantage continuously move
in favour of the ADCs.

Private traders and multinationals located in the LDCs have
shown a tendency to prefer imports in order to supply the compara-
tively rich urban elites with foreign luxury goods. Such imports
have set into motion domestic production of socially unnecessary
goods and raise expectations unsuited to the needs of the LDCs.

> Such tendencies would not only be socially divisive but they
> would divert scarce foreign exchange from socially desirable
> investment to luxury consumption. Instead China, and the
> like-minded countries pursue a basic policy of economic self-
> sufficiency and export only in order to be able to import
> 'socially desirable products' (basically capital items and if
> necessary, food) when there is a marked advantage in the
> exchange. [6]

Few of the ADC countries plan their trade strategies on the basis
of trade theory but they often use the theoretical argument to tell the
LDCs that any attempt to adopt 'inward looking policies' would go
against the theory of maximizing welfare from trade, without
saying much about the problems of unequal exchange, exploitative
nature of trade, protectionism, export pessimism or unfairness in
technological exports, i.e. by concealing the trading bases for
Darwinism which are summarized below.

1. It can be statistically shown that the distribution gains from trade
are now almost wholly biased against the LDCs for a variety of
reasons, the most important being that the very strong institutions
of international economic order and international trading regimes
are controlled by the ADCs. More important movements in international prices are very much exogamously determined for the
LDCs.[7]

---

[6] Colman and Nixen, *Economics of Change in Less Developed Countries*, op. cit.,
1978, p. 85.

[7] Norman Gemmell, ed., *Surveys in Development Economics*, T.J. Press, Padstow,
Great Britain.

2. By and large international trade is causing, instead of removing, underdevelopment at the periphery, particularly by the new trend towards increase of trade barriers. The contradiction between the pressure of mainstream theory towards freer trade on the one hand and new trade barriers on the other make the LDCs vulnerable.[8]

3. The trade theories which assume that entry into trade allows a country to employ previously surplus productive capacity, which existed because of lack of domestic substitutability, have failed to find empirical support. In fact, the argument of surplus capacities can be used both for and against trade.[9]

4. A very strong argument against the prevailing trade patterns stems from the fact that entry into trade makes a sizeable element of productive capacity vulnerable to external disturbances because production cannot be easily switched from export to domestic markets.[10]

5. In a majority of cases it has been shown that the dominant trade theories, if followed, tend to reduce the rate of growth (compared with autarky) in a country exporting agricultural products. The possibility of non-mutually beneficial trade that arises from static principles of comparative advantage is derived from the mainstream of trade theories, from Ricardo to Heckscher-Ohlin. The famous Stopler-Samuelson Theorem, which assumes that trade benefits the abundant factor, which in the LDCs is labour, has not proved correct because the domestic labour markets are often neither competitive nor efficient. Moreover, trade restrictions benefit the scarce factor according to the Stopler-Samuelson Theorem.[11]

6. The most critical impact of trade on the LDCs has been negative and defined as 'immiserizing or welfare lowering' by way of increased output turning the terms of trade against the growing countries. Terms of trade losses more than offset the positive production and consumption effect on trade expansion, as shown by Bhagwati: immiserization can be due to distortions and failures

[8] S. Amin, *Unequal Development*, Harvester Press, Brighton, 1976.

[9] R.E. Caves, 'Vent for surplus models of trade and growth', in R.E. Baldwin *et al.* (eds), *Trade, Growth and the Balance of Payments*, Ran McNally, Chicago, 1965.

[10] J.N. Bhagwati and T.N. Srinivasan, 'Trade Policy and Development', in R. Dornbusch and J.A. Frenkel (eds), *International Economic Policy: Theory and Evidence*, Johns Hopkins University Press, Baltimore, 1979.

[11] H.W. Singer, 'The distribution of gains from trade and investment—revisited. *Journal of Development Studies*, II, pp. 376-82.

to equalize domestic and foreign rates of transformation.[12]

7. The intra-industry trade is predominantly observed in the high-income countries. It remains stunted in the LDCs' manufacturing industries due to the absence of forward and backward linkages.Besides, relative endowments and country size factors may restrict intra-industry trade in manufactures with respect to North-South relations.[13]

8. The entire stream of international trade theories ultimately falls back on the so-called 'second best'. This proposition has been used extensively for violating trade principles and using them against the LDCs.[14]

9. Nothing has made reliance on trade more suspect than the argument of 'trade pessimism'. The pessimism is due to (i) decline in the terms of trade of primary producers vis-à-vis those of manufacturing goods producers resulting in a long-term transfer of income from developing to developed countries; (ii) the lower income elasticity of demand for primary products than for manufacturing goods imposing lower growth on the LDCs; (iii) secular tendencies towards payment deficits, currency depreciation, and terms of trade deterioration of the LDCs; and (iv) demographic pressure which prohibits taking out productivity gain in the form of higher wages, particularly in the face of falling relative prices of exportables.[15]

10. The filling up of two gaps, the external trade gap and the internal savings investment gap, as required by the application of growth assumption, failed to materialize. When growth is constrained by domestic savings and the gap is to be filled by foreign aid, the success of such a model depends upon many factors, such as the right kind of import substitution, export promotion, factor substitutability. Only a few countries such as Korea and Taiwan conformed to this model; others did not.

The aforementioned assumptions, facts and theories, which sug-

[12] J.N. Bhagwati, 'The pure theory of international trade: a survey', *Economic Journal*, 74, 1964, pp. 1-8.

[13] D. Greenaway and C.R. Milner, 'Effective tariff analysis for Burundi', *A Study of the Tariff System in Burundi*, A report to the World Bank, Maxwell Stamp Associates, London, 1986.

[14] D. Sapsford, 'The statistical debate on the net barter terms of trade: a comment and some additional information', *Economic Journal*, 95, 1985, pp. 781-88.

[15] H.B. Chenery and A. Strout, 'Foreign assistance and economic development', *American Economic Review*, 56, 1966, pp. 679-733.

gest that the international economic system is heavily loaded against the South, make nonsense of all those trade theories which have been recommended to the LDCs. The various gaps mentioned above have strengthened the existing dualism between the ADCs and LDCs. Internal and external dualism reinforce each other to pro-duce a Darwinist impasse. We have seen how the LDCs have been reduced to the level of just a periphery in four decades and are being pushed out of the global decision-making system. The option of delinking from this system has become the central strategy of the LDCs or the South.

But there would be at least two big shouts against this approach. One will come from the protagonists of the interdependence theory. How can there be, even if one wills it, detachment in a world that is shrinking because of growing interdependence? These arguments need not be taken seriously, for after all it can be shown that the world would be most neatly knit into interdependence through straight forward imperialism. No one will escape it. The other shout is worth more serious consideration. How can a country detach itself from the rest of the world in the field of science and technology and capital and hope to remain both powerful and independent?

Gonnatilke has suggested two most appropriate paths: first, detach and then reattach; second, transcend the links. The second is the necessary condition for the first to be fixed. Transcending means creating an entirely new social and economic base for science and technology. The scientific community will have to be organized around a rethought out development strategy. The social context of science will need reorientation in terms of the past and the future. After all there were good traditions of science and society before independence in countries like India. We have to first shift from the feudal to the mercantilist view of science and technology before we reach an industrial view of it. Transcendence would mean its spread from the physical sciences to the social sciences. It means a social revolution.

Delinking from the ADCs will require strengthening links within the LDCs. If South-South cooperation has come to nothing, it is primarily due to the dependence of the LDCs on the ADCs for finance and technology, and due to the successful strategy of the ADCs to keep the LDCs divided. The fact that almost all the wars fought since 1954 were fought among the LDCs, with borrowed weaponry from the ADCs, shows how difficult the process of South-South cooperation is. To link together all the LDCs is impossible for a variety of reasons.

There are two possibilities. First, the LDCs will have to be grouped regionally, ideologically (democracies for instance), or otherwise to form international regimes with minimum internal fights and contradictions. If the global order is dominated by international regimes in the military, political and economic fields, the LDCs cannot carve a place for themselves without using the same kind of instruments. Some like the ASEAN and the Gulf Cooperation Council have made a good beginning but if other LDCs do not regroup themselves, the danger is that the middle-income LDCs will get more easily integrated in a relative dependency situation with the ADCs, leaving others to be Darwinized first.

The main burden of cooperation will be on the large countries like India, Mexico, Brazil, Nigeria and Algeria. Once this kind of international regime emerges, cooperation with some middle powers within the ADCs may be possible. The Kualalumpur meeting of 15 LDCs in July 1990 marked the right beginning but unfortunately the meeting fell into many old traps.

Whatever the difficulties and prospects for South-South cooperation, it is incumbent on large-size LDCs like India, Mexico, Brazil, Nigeria and Algeria to change their entire development strategy. It is no ordinary change and even if one had a model of change it will be to remove the burden of external dependence and the illusion that without foreign capital development is not possible. What was once historically valued is no longer so, at least for the Darwinized nations.

Though there has always been a strong plea made for South-South cooperation, the way in which the whole scheme was conceived was unrealistic. Even the ADCs, which have set up several institutions for explicit international macro-economic policy cooperation, do not find it easy to cooperate. The ADCs' economic system has a structural force to make policy-makers converge towards optimal solutions. There is more implicit than explicit coordination. A concrete example was recently provided by a group of economists working for the Brookings Institution. They asked those responsible for the twelve leading econometric models of the world economy to simulate the effects of some carefully specified policy changes. The results were only marginally different in the positive direction from the non-cooperative equilibrium in which each government sets its policies while taking those of the others as given. The positive results were subject to new qualifications which are not likely to be fulfilled. The maximum advantage goes to the country which can discover the true model and not through coordination. The whole exercise seems dismal.[16]

Yet, if it is sufficiently realized that some partial de-linking from international trade regimes is essential then there has to be an entirely new domestic development strategy and a new kind of self-reliance. To avoid serious dislocation this strategy will also aim at (i) maintaining foreign exchange earnings by investments in selective areas, and (ii) saving and reducing the use of foreign exchange by maximum mobilization and exploitation of domestic resources through a new set of transformation strategies. The main purpose would be to avoid external deficits through a course different from the so-called strategy of import substitution which has increased rather than decreased external obligations.

Second, one may not have much faith in the conscience of the so-called international community, but to wish it away is to get self-Darwinized. Almost the entire system of international regimes is controlled by governments of nation-states, more than two-thirds of which are dictatorships of one kind and another. The more sensitive and committed elite of the LDCs should therefore give the highest priority in their approach towards a new global order to the creation of such international bodies for development that are outside governmental control.

The LDCs are now faced with a cruel dilemma. They have not challenged the essential structure of the international system. They have only demanded some distribution of wealth and power within the system. They have respected the state system in general, notwithstanding the fact that they were exploited and repressed by the nation-states system. As Tucker has argued: 'It is primarily through the state that the historically oppressed and disadvantaged nations seek to mount a successful challenge to what governing elites of developing countries view as persisting unjust inequalities.' And this approach had a fatal flaw.[17]

The dilemma is that the LDCs can no longer fight the inequalities of the international system through their own nation-state system. They have no power to challenge the existing system either in economic or in military terms. Whatever their character, the third world nation-states are in fact an instrument of domination, though

---

[16] Brookings Institution, Washington, 1986.
[17] Robert W. Tucker, *America in Decline*, p. 471.

in their own eyes they are a defence mechanism against domination.

Reform of the international system should be towards joint representation of governments and non-government bodies, such as in the IIO. The most important reform for which the LDCs must strive is to demand democratization of the UNsystem by suggesting the creation of secondchambers, at least in the functional agencies dealing with development issues. Once upon a time a giant international authority for development aid was mooted but the proposal was shot down by the existing international agencies, simply because the idea behind the proposal was to break the monopoly of agencies that represent and are controlled by government.

The whole UN system, particularly its functional agencies which were designed to influence economic development, are controlled by the representatives of governments who often act against their own people. Indeed, the UN is the biggest barrier in the way of creating a new international economic order. Many a person believes that unless the UN is reformed or replaced by different kinds of reorganizations there is not much hope for the LDCs, either in respect of economic development or in respect of peace and security.

Third, the debate has to move from the economic to the moral side, as it is an integral part of a Gandhian paradigm. For instance, the most critical problem that many LDCs face is that of the growing burden of international debt. Despite various schemes to reduce this burden the total debt obligation is increasing. Short of total or partial cancellation, there can be no solution of the debt problem either within the prevailing international financial system or by schemes of reduction which do not tackle the fundamental causes arising out of the domination syndrome. Indeed, international debt has become a moral problem. It is moral in the sense that both the creditor and debtor governments and institutions have to yield their privileges and agree to the cancellation of the debt in a way that hurts most those who have illegally transferred funds from the LDCs to the ADCs. More importantly, the funds acquired through cancellation have to be put in non-governmental international bodies with the clear mandate to use all the funds for the removal of poverty and the upliftment of the weaker sections. This may sound impractical to hardcore mainstream economists but in the absence of imbibing the moral dimensions of the problem there can be no solution. There is some realization of the moral issues among some western economists, but their voices are weak.[18] Ironically, the ruling elites of the LDCs object to this scheme as much as the creditors, but a strong non-violent international movement could create pressures towards a realistic solution.

Fourth, contrary to the general impression and easy acceptance of the theory of imperialism, most of the LDCs, except the OPEC nations and a few others, are extremely deficient in natural resources. Moreover, the ADCs have increasingly opted for technology-oriented man-made substitutes for raw materials. But saving the nature and ecology demand immediate cooperation. Therefore, the LDCs, in their own interests, must demand pooling of sovereignties in respect of areas of ecology, raw materials, and above all those old and new technologies which the ADCs can use for global control.

Fifth, since most of the LDCs are run by dictatorships of one kind or another, it is now largely accepted that the struggle for democracy and human rights is inseparable from that of achieving economic independence, removal of poverty, reduction of inequalities, etc. Even in the LDC democracies, corruption and state-sponsored repression are undermining constitutionally guaranteed rights. One of the reasons why the leaders of the LDCs prefer the prevailing global system is the fear of losing their dictatorial power and vast economic wealth, most of which they have accumulated illegally. The LDCs will find numerous allies in the ADCs in this struggle.

In general, it would be a mistake not to use or exploit the prevailing order without falling into its trap as theorists of dependency, interdependence or imperialism have done so far. There is a lot of scope to undermine the system from within. What has been suggested above is not a simple list of policies or strategies. When integrated, the suggestions constitute a new and alternative paradigm. There is a new consensus among political economists, particularly articulated by philosophers like Kuhn, Lakatos and Popper, that behind all the apparently conflicting schools of economic thought, there is the force of a western paradigm which has entrenched the global divide between the ADCs and the LDCs.

---

[18] Arjo Klmer, 'The Conversation with Amrita Sen', *Journal of Economic Perspective*, Winter 1989; and R.D. Winfred, *The Just Economy*, Routledge, London, 1988, p. 1.

Most models of growth were borrowed from the ADCs' inbuilt force towards Darwinizing the LDCs. Change has become imperative and necessary for those elites who wish to maintain their independence. Such a strategy will require new approaches to technology and ecology and new social formations. One may find some allies in the ADCs in this struggle. For instance, if full employment, ecological balance, and relevant technology are put in the centre of things, or made forces of national development and international struggle, the scenario can change internationally as well.

The most significant change in the domestic strategy of development will require a shift of focus from the growth rate to some other important variable. Many economists and international organizations have suggested a shift to employment because the earlier shifts from growth to development and basic needs strategy have not succeeded, largely because the new strategies were treated as adjuncts of the growth rate. The central point is that the growth rate has to be derived and be the outcome of other strategies rather than their determinant. This is a difficult concept and even more difficult to put into operation, but there is no escape. The old determinate requirements for a high growth rate, such as high savings rate, filling of two gaps, availability of technology and skills, etc. have been satisfied in many LDCs, and yet with a few exceptions, the majority of the LDCs have failed to grow faster.

It is not possible to go into the structure and details of alternative strategies. What can be done at best is to enumerate them. Four strategies have to be integrated to evolve a new paradigm of development. These are: (i) employment, (ii) national and international food security system, (iii) shift from welfare state to human resource development State, (iv) appropriate technology choices. The pursuit of these strategies, both independently and in relation to one another would ultimately result in enhanced growth rate. The earlier notion that only a high rate of accumulation can produce a high growth rate has proved to be false. Nor is it any more accepted that the growth rate will go down with these strategies.

So far the notions of imports have been guided by three factors: (i) rising expectations; (ii) catching up with the ADCs; and (iii) the ADCs' consumerism. The LDCs have been obliged to structure their domestic production to meet the pressures of these three economic considerations. These preferred philosophies have led to wholesale reliance on imported machines, technologies, management, finance and even food and raw materials. All this has to be reversed. Self-reliance means, as Gandhi said, self-respect and self-determination of strategies. Echoing Gandhi, W. Schwendler has suggested to the LDCs, separately and collectively:

> If development is to fulfil people's expectations it cannot be patterned on an outside model; it must be achieved in accordance with goals and methods freely chosen by each society, care being taken to ensure that exchange of knowledge in the social and human sciences, as also technology, do not impede endogenous development but on the contrary, help it get off the ground.[19]

The most fundamental reform in the international system that can save the LDCs from Darwinization is that the UN and all its functional agencies such as FAO, UNESCO, ILO, etc., must be reformed in a way in which the government representatives and non-government representatives have equal power of debating and decision-making. At present the entire international system is run by committees of government representatives. There is not even a semblance of participation by non-government representatives, except at ILO. Non-governmental experts are simply coopted by the UN and other agencies and are well paid to play the convenient game of those who have monopolised the international system. It is important, therefore, that the UN and other functional agencies should have two chambers, one representing the government and the other representing the people. The proposal might seem difficult to put into operation, but it is not impossible. The proposal should be high on the agenda because government representatives of the LDCs have already joined in conspiracy with the ADCs and are no longer interested in liberating their own poeple. To begin with, development strategies will have to be discussed at official and non-official levels. But both levels will have to have equal powers.

Finally, as far as I know, no economist in India or abroad has ever used the concept of *dumping of industries* as the greatest threat to the LDCs. In 1931, during the Depression years representatives of Indian business went to see Gandhi and complained about the

---

[19] For further elaboration see, Lynden Moore, *Growth and Structure of International Trade since Second World War*, Heartsheaf Books, Sussex, 1985.

dumping of goods by Japan and other developed countries. Gandhi warned them that the problems that the poor nations would face when they become independent would not be dumping of goods but dumping of second-rate industries, and that is precisely what has happened. He added that the day Unilever becomes Hindustan Lever, that would be the ruin of India. India has signed 14,000 collaborations and in most cases the technologies are second-rate and uncompetitive. Darwinism will prevail if technological dependence continues.[20]

I have suggested above a few lines of direction along which, to use a Gandhian phrase, 'an international non-violent and non-cooperation movement' may start. In my forthcoming book, *Global Economic Crises and the Gandhian Response*, the strategies for resistance and cooperation strategies that the LDCs need have been fully detailed.

---

[20] *Harijan*, March 26, 1931. Also see Appendix.

TOWARDS AN ALTERNATIVE
PARADIGM – III

International Debt Is a Moral Problem

No other problem expresses sharply the global disorder as the debt burden on the LDCs. The burden of the debt is so large and its servicing so arduous that it is practically wrecking the financial linkages between the ADCs and LDCs. At one level it may seem to be establishing a relationship between the two but at a more deeper level it is fracturing their relations. The global debt has crossed the figure of 1200 billion dollars. Only three years ago it was less than 1000 billion dollars. It is estimated that even if all the proposed schemes for reduction of the burden of these debts are sincerely put into operation, the structure of this debt and the global financial system are such that not only will the overall burden remain the same, it must inevitably increase. There is a lot of hue and cry from some of the debtor countries, but it is both a cry in the wilderness and a cry by hypocrites.

Several schemes and plans have been put forward to solve the debt burden problem. Most of these schemes have come either from the international financial institutions or from the representatives of the developed countries. Some were suggested by third world leaders who went back on them as soon as pressure mounted. For instance, in 1985 Alan Garcia, President of Peru, announced that he would not devote more than 10 per cent of his country's export to serve debt. He said, 'It is either debt or democracy.' Several Latin American countries seem to endorse that goal, but the harshness of the economic system did not permit this threat to materialize. Since the creditor countries are very powerful, they can always seriously hurt the debtor countries one way or the other if the latter try to renege on their obligations.

In fact the response of the creditor nations has been to offer such relief plans by means of which if the debt burden was partially reduced it correspondingly increased the degree of dependence of the LDCs in some other form. It is a problem of the capacity to exercise power rather than of conformity to rules of international law. After all, Britain and France defaulted in payment to the US during the 1930s on the grounds that their obligations to meet the needs of the people were greater than the legal obligations to creditors.

There are several questions that are being asked. First, is it possible to cancel a part of the debt one way or the other? Second, is it possible to reduce the burden of the interest payment by lowering the interest rates? Third, can the international financial institutions take up the responsibility to manage the debt in the interests of both the creditors and the debtors? In fact, these were the questions to which the Baker and the Brady, the IMF and the World Bank have attempted short-range responses but without much success. Correctly, each scheme was designed to bail out one country at a time.

Is there a Gandhian solution to the problem? In my view there is a solution if only one can honestly answer the question whether global debt is an economic issue only, or whether it has become a moral issue? If debt is treated purely as an economic or financial issue without straightaway its cancellation in part or whole, then there is no solution. At best only schemes for alleviation of the burden can be proposed. However, once the global debt is treated as a moral problem as well, then the answer becomes different and indeed cancellation is given the form that is fair to all parties except those who have illegally profited from the debt. Thus, it is the moral responsibility of all concerned to eliminate the parasitic class first and then come to a final settlement problem. Indeed, the principle of morality might have to replace partially the principle of financial liability and economic equity in the entire global economic order.

The direction in which the negotiations for re-ordering the trade and investment regimes are going on, suggests that the scope for repayment even by large exporters from the developing countries, let alone the others, is extremely limited. For instance, Brazil which had an 18 billion dollar export surplus last year has no money to pay this year. The liberalization which is being imposed on all these countries by the international organizations on the one hand and the trading policies of the advanced developed countries (ADCs) on the other are likely to worsen the situation further. The worsening terms of trade, the declining proportion of the share of global trade, the trend towards reverse transfer payments, raising of protection walls and almost total dependence for sophisticated weapons on the big military powers, etc., all point towards greater and not smaller debt and other obligations imposed on the LDCs.

The irony is that the more the LDCs tried to export, the less became their share in global trade. The more they tried to import capital and machinery for an increasing domestic manufacturing base, including that from exports, the less was their share in global manufacture. The more they relied on import of technology, the wider was the gap between the ADCs and the LDCs, and so on. The trade figures expose these anomalies. In the last one decade the share of the LDCs in global trade has declined from 15 per cent to 9.5 per cent, if we exclude the gang of four and the OPEC countries. No one is claiming that there is a possibility of reversal of these trends.

No wonder, the larger the transfer of resources the greater is the burden of debt repayment. Indeed, during the last few years, despite increasing gross transfers, the net transfers have become negative. What has been happening is the recycling of old debts. Financial development in the ADCs revealed tenuous relations and marginal concern with the problems of the LDCs. The latter make practically no contribution to the billions of dollars of daily transactions that take place in the financial markets in LDCs. Indeed, contrary to the general impression, the financial markets of the ADCs and LDCs have very few linkages. There is a complete rupture between the two.

The conditions which facilitated the creation of debt have changed so much that repayment had become impossible. Global debt was the most ironic consequence of the hike in oil prices which created a bonaza for some and crisis for others. The oil companies and the international institutions managed to collect and recycle all the petro-dollars. They allured both the creditors and debtors by dividing their ranks. The LDCs were pushed into the debt trap as much by these organizations as by the greed of their own ruling elites who thought that they had got an easy opening for capital offered at low interest rates and long-term maturity instead of mobilizing their own resources and people for development. After the fall in the price of oil since the 1980s, two things happened. The surplus petro-dollars disappeared. The debtor countries thought that manna was falling from the heavens which they would never be required to repay and that they would also be able to borrow indefinitely. They landed themselves in a total mess and new dependency.

The banking system is naturally worried, but not too much. It is flush with hot money and junk bonds which are the new commodities in the international market. One thing is sure, that all those who hoped for or feared a repeat of the 1929-31 crash have been forced to hide their tail between their legs. There is going to be no monetary crash because nearly 6 trillion dollars of hot money is floating in the markets of Tokyo, London and New York to correct any deviant situation. Even though a growing share of corporate income is being absorbed in interest payments, there is no chance of the liquidity position seriously deteriorating. Indeed, reliance on short-term debt is increasing so much that long-term and short-term markets are getting segmented, making things very confusing for the LDCs.

In what sense is the problem more moral than financial? It is a well-known fact that a large part of the LDCs' debt was transferred in one form or the other back to the creditor nations through illegal means. In Brazil it is openly stated that the sum of 120 billion dollars that Brazil owes to the international system is almost equal to the amount illegally transferred and lying with the Miami and other banks. The same is true of the one-party government in Mexico which has a debt of 98 billion dollars, but it is believed that its elite classes have 56 billion dollars in external accounts.

The shift of aid from communities to governments only led to conspiracies between the bureaucracies of the donor and receiver nations. According to Prof. C.F. Murray, 'this new bandit is officially called "Institutional Building". The earlier 1960s approach was denounced as imperialist but the then third-world elite who gave this slogan pocketed the funds, primarily transferred funds to Mercedes Benz and Swiss Bank accounts.'

The debt problem was partly the product of debtors' willingness to fall into the trap of the international economic system and the policies of a get-rich-quick leadership. As the London *Economist* observed, 'overseas bankers persuaded, cajoled or bribed countries like Nigeria into taking their hands off the surplus oil money they were desperately trying to recycle'. Some of the major debtors are rich oil-producing nations: Mexico, Brazil, Nigeria, Indonesia. But all of them have corrupt governments and most of what they earned from the oil bonaza of 1973 onwards did not go towards the right kind of development or for the starving poor. It was pocketed by the corrupt elite. It is well known that Nigeria earned more than 100 billion dollars between 1973-1981, a sum which would have been enough to turn the nation into a first-rate economy, but it was squandered. When the oil prices tumbled the oil-producing debtors were ruined. Besides, large amounts of money had been siphoned off to Swiss and British banks. The non-oil producing LDCs were ruined at the hands of both.

Urgent appeals and even schemes for treating more fairly such special cases as the African debt have been issued without effect. In reality there is no way out under the prevailing dispensation. Political pressures by the LDCs have weakened considerably. Organizations like NAM and Group 77 have become defunct. Above all, the ruling elites of the LDCs live in such luxury, both at home and abroad, that they do not evoke any sympathy on economic considerations.

The moral dimension of the problem is that both the debtors and creditors must pay the price but not the suffering and poor masses. Only those who grabbed and transferred funds illegally and those international institutions which benefit from such transfers should be obliged to pay.

The following proposals are suggestions for the alleviation of the debt burden and the final elimination of debt. It must, however, be kept in mind that these proposals do not uniformly apply to all the LDCs, as the situation differs from country to country.

First, the ADC governments and banks have to gradually absorb both the interest and the capital burden of the debt with two assurances. One, future debts will be given on some self-liquidating principle. That does not concern us here. The second is more important. The accounts liquidated will be put in a separate fund and will not fall into the hands either of the existing creditors or debtors.

The second proposal was well bugun within the poorest nations. There should be a new international agency which will guarantee repayment of all loans on the condition that the interest payments are done away with. This agency will get new funds from donors as well as from debtors. The crucial condition is that this agency will not consist of the representatives of LDC governments. Instead, on its Board of Directors will be the representatives of specially created non-governmental development bodies of both ADCs and LDCs. Some representatives of international financial institutions could be there as guarantors.

Third, as is clear from past experience, governments of LDCs which are dictatorial and corrupt are unlikely to make the best use of the new resources. Hence only those LDCs will be given debt relief which will create autonomous non-governmental development bodies. The possibility will always remain of such bodies being manipulated but it should not be difficult to monitor and evaluate their work by the international body suggested above.

Fourth, the proposed international agency will also be authorized to charge interest rates, give interest-free loans or make grants, change the maturity pattern of the debt, create conversion schemes and issue new securities, etc. These will be done in relation to both the ability of the borrower to pay and the commitment tothe new task of development equity.

If the aforementioned conditions are fulfilled, the problem of the removal of the debt burden moves from the economic to the moral plane. The debt burden will be reduced with the help of new money but this money will be used for the development of the weaker sections. It will not be allowed to become a part of the normal elite controlled development strategy. But the real burden is not only debt, but the big economic legacy of trade deficits left over from the time when debt and oil earnings created such structural distortions in the economy that trade deficit became inevitable. Indeed, reduction of the debt burden will have to be accompanied by an entirely new strategy of development.

TOWARDS AN ALTERNATIVE
PARADIGM – IV

Mahatma's Theory of Dumping
of Industries

I

There are two objectives for writing this Chapter. The first is to bring to the notice of the economist and other concerned scholars the important concept of Dumping of Industries which Mahatma Gandhi used 58 years ago, a concept which has been neglected and which Gandhi was the only one to have ever used it. To my knowledge no one from Adam Smith to Karl Marx to Keynes to Dependency Theorists ever thought of it, notwithstanding the fact that it conformed to reality as nearly as was possible. Most of the third world's industrialization has been thwarted precisely by import substitution which relied on the import of technologies or turn-key second rate industries.

Second, next to trade, if not preceding it, the area in which the LDCs have let themselves be marginalized is that of manufacturing industry. Even India which had considerable industrial experience, let alone other developing nations which did not have such experience, failed to hear Gandhi's clear warning that it was in the borrowed pattern of industrialization that the LDCs could be defeated on their home ground. He feared and warned against what he called the Dumping of Industries by the ADCs through many allurements, Somehow the ruling elites of the LDCs were made to believe that they could industrialize in a rather short time if only they followed the west, had access to western capital and technology and if they were to enter into collaboration agreements with western companies, particularly multinationals.

It is ironic that the LDC leaders like Nehru rather treated with indifference if not contempt the Japanese and Korean response to the same western allurements in protecting themselves by a variety of methods and heading western multinationals at their own game. The latter well understood the danger of dumping of industries and at each stage of their industrialization built a variety of safety sets. They triumphed whereas others failed, and failed so massively that there is little of hope of their industrialization on a competitive basis.

Let me first explain the concept of dumping of industries and context in which it was coined. Gandhi coined this concept during the years of the great depression of the thirties in the context of foreign goods being dumped in India. During the depression year cheap European and Japanese goods were sold in the Indian market at prices below the costs and consequently hundreds of units, particularly, the small ones went bankrupt. Even before all this happened Gandhi had given a call for Swedishi which was a part of his grand model of Poorna Swaraj. Without full Swadeshi, India could not enter the international market, Gandhi elaborately argued, just as without village industries India could not fully develop her villages. Indeed along with Truth and Non-violence these concepts encompass practically all aspects of man's freedom and liberation, be it an individual, social group, a nation or an international order.

To have Gandhiji's authoritative opinion on this matter and his definition of Swadeshi industries, three representatives of the Scindia Steam Navigation Company had an interview with him some time in March 1931 and asked him the questions about the discrimination clauses in the new constitution.

Gandhi had earlier written an article in *Young India* entitled 'The Giant and the Dwarf' in which he had said: 'To talk of no discrimination between Indian interests and English or European is to perpetuate Indian as hostage. What is equality of rights between a giant and a dwarf? Before one can think of equality between unequals, the dwarf must be raised to the height of the giant. . . It will be a misnomer to call the process one of racial discrimination. There is no such question. There is room enough in our country for every British man, woman and child if they will shed their privileged position and share our lot'.[1]

And again: 'In almost every walk of life the Englishman by reason of his belonging to the ruling class occupies a privileged position. It can be said without fear of contradiction and without exaggeration that he has risen upon the ruin of India's commerce and industries. The cottage industries of India had to perish in order that Lancashire might flourish.'[2]

The industrial representatives asked what were Indian or Swadeshi companies? He replied, 'what are Indian or Swadeshi Companies? It has become a fashion nowadays to bamboozle the unwary public by adding '(India) Limited' to full-blooded British concerns. Lever Brothers '(India) Limited' have their factories here now. They claim to produce Swadeshi soaps, and have already ruined several large and small soap factories in Bengal. Then there is the Imperial (India) Ltd. which has received valuable concessions. *This is dumping foreign industries instead of foreign goods on us'*.

'Then there are companies with Indian Directorate with British Managing Agents who direct the Directorate. Would you call a company with a large percentage of Indian capital and a large number of Indian Directors on the Board, but with a non-Indian Managing Director or non-Indian film as Managing Agents, a Swadeshi concern?'

The Mahatma made two other points to the representatives of the industry. Both statements are quite remarkable and express the acute understanding of the industries:

'As regards the definition of a Swadeshi Company, I would say that only those concerns can be regarded as Swadeshi whose control, direction and management, either by a Managing Director or by Managing Agents, are in Indian hands. I should have no objection to the use of Foreign capital, or to the employment of foreigners—but only on condition that such capital and such talents are exclusively under the control, direction and management of Indians and are used in the interests of India'.

'But the use of foreign capital or talent is one thing, and the dumping of foreign industries concerns is totally another thing. The concerns you have named cannot in the remotest sense of the terms be called Swadeshi. Rather than countenance of these ventures, I would prefer the development of the industries in question

[1] *Harijan*, March 26, 1931.
[2] Ibid.

to be delayed by a few years in order to permit national capital and enterprise to grow up and build such industries in future under the actual control, direction and management of Indians themselves.'[3]

LDCs have no industrial future if they do not fight back dumping of industries that comes through a variety of doors—import of technology, foreign aid and import substitution, trade and above all foreign collaborations. If for the last four decades, newly independent poor nations failed to face the challenges of industrialization, it was largely because of their ruling elites who tried to imitate the West or the East and thereby succumbed to pursuing development strategies which turned out to be inimical to development itself. One such policy was about the import of technologies and finance to support industrialization. Technologies were made available, but seldom were these technologies either relevant to resource endowment or always the latest. More importantly, what has been noticed is that through technology, finance and management the ADCs dumped on the LDC old industries which totally distorted their development perspectives. Mahatma Gandhi had warned against these possibilities. But no attention was paid to his warnings. Unless a new policy framework is structured, even if it meant dismantling parts of the existing industries, there is no hope for the ADCs. Foreign capital or technologies cannot be taken in abstract.

For decades we have been shouting from house tops phrases such as national self-reliance, collective self-reliance, or their opposites which are summed up in Dependence Theory or some version of Neocolonialism. In reality the experience of the development decades and development theories and strategies has been very bitter. Despite good intentions things have gone topsy-turvy because many of the policies suggested for acquiring self-reliance or economic autonomy ended up producing exactly the opposite effect. Most theories were borrowed, were misfit or misconceived as were technologies and capital goods and other industries.

All this was not the result of faulty implementation as is often stated. It was realised, though quite late, that the borrowed models for development from outside were misconceived and were actually instruments of new colonialism. Both faulty models and inefficient implementation pushed the poor nations into a trap of dependence and stagnation from which they are unable to get out

[3] Ibid.

now. India was loudest proclaimant of self-reliance and now unfortunately represents the picture of most glaring dependence or one openly denied high-tech imports.

One of the reasons for this state of affairs has been policies relating to role of foreign capital, technology and management along with foreign aid in Indian Industrial Development. Not even the ardent nationalists ever suggested that there should be no reliance on foreign components as there was inevitable import content of the development, only if the maximization of the development content of imports could be ensured all the time. It is not possible to go into other aspects of industrial policy which have contributed to slow down of the industrial growth and its distortions. The focus will remain on only one aspect of the foreign capital, collaboration agreements, aid or technology. It is in this context that the concept of Dumping of Industries will be analysed.

Although it did not come to me as a surprise though it has surprised many economists that Mahatma Gandhi who was not a trained economist had a more acute sense of self-reliance and understanding of all related economic issues than the so called trained economists of then and today had. No one before or after him has spoken of threat of dumping of industries as distinguished from dumping of goods. Second rate technologies and third rate industries are being dumped on the Third World as a part of the de-industrialization of old industries in the developed world. It is amazing that both the developing nations and the international system are expecting these rejected industries to be used for export promotion.

For Gandhi such concepts as import substitution, export promotion were of secondary importance. More important was the explicit discrimination between India and foreign industrialists which was brazenly practised by the British and which for no rational reasons Nehru insisted to continue. He insisted on the reverse of what Gandhi advocated. This point was also ignored by our leaders who came with and after Nehru. Important substitution, an approach accepted more or less by every third world economist or nation, while widening the production base of manufacturing has pushed developing nations into a new dependence, debt trap and stagnation from which they cannot get out. Ironically, the few cases where import substitution was successful and autonomy achieved were those which combined with export aggressiveness, as for instance in Japan, Korea, Taiwan, etc. or by making both import substitution and export promotion subservient to a general plan of autonomous development, as was for instance in China, in which imports were planned to fill the gap between domestic needs and supplies.

The aforementioned or any other idea, theory or concept put forward by Gandhi can only be realized within his conceptual framework and specific context. The threat of dumping industries was evolved at the time and in the context of the great depression of the thirties as well as a problem of dependency. Swadeshi and Swaraj are the two central concepts of Mahatma Gandhi. Along with Truth and Non-violence they encompass practically all aspects of freedom and liberation, be it of a social group or a nation or even of an individual.

Nehru also talked about self-reliance but without ever giving an adequate definition of it, so much so that much of external economic relations only led to a new colonization even through new industries came up. Indeed, one can draw a distinct dividing line between Gandhi's concept of Swadeshi and Nehru's imitation model that was given the name of self-reliance. Incidentally this latter concept was adopted by most of the third world nations and their record has been even more dismal. Nehru seldom used either of the Gandhian concepts because both had an internal policy implication unacceptable to Nehru.

According to Reserve Bank survey of foreign collaborations of 1985: 'The basic policy of the Government of India in regard to foreign private investment continues to be based on the cardinal principles mentioned in the statement made in April 1949, by the late Prime Minister Nehru in Parliament. The uppermost consideration underlying the policy statement were non-discrimination between an Indian and a foreign enterprise and larger interests of the country. These principles were incorporated in the Industrial Policy Resolution of 1956.'

Probably the most disastrous decision ever taken by Mr. Nehru in respect of foreign capital was in 1949 when through two laws an Industrial Policy Resolution and policy statement on foreign capital in respect of Government policies and thus stopped the liquidation of the British colonial capital. From 1945 to 1949 the British capitalists were selling their enterprises to Indians at almost throw away prices. That phase could be described as a beginning of economic decolonisation in India. From 1949 onwards began a slow and steady re-colonisation, ironically under the banner of plan-

ning, self-reliance and foreign aid. A delegation led by Sir Parshot-
amdas Thakurdas, the most distinguished nationalist industrial
entrepreneur, met Nehru and begged of him to let the British
liquidate the capital before new policy on foreign capital was
announced. They even suggested to him that if he did not like the
Indian businessmen, let the Government take over the British
capital. But Nehru brushed aside their remonstrations and recom-
mendations. Those two particular economic policy resolutions of
1949 laid the basis of India's march towards dependence, semi-
compradoism right through industrialization and diversification.

All that was required of the foreign companies was to change the
share of equity capital and the managerial personnel between
Indian and foreign citizens. All this was later defined as the so
called FERA law which helped the foreigners to compete with
Indian firms on equal terms. It was not realised that a country
emerging from colonialism with foreign capital dominating and
having practically no capital goods industry, could not have adopted
a more self-damaging industrial policy. The British investors who
were leaving and selling their industrial enterprises were not
producers of capital goods but this aspect was totally lost on Nehru.
Unfortunately the Marxist economists and the Communists followed a sectarian line, raised a banner of revolt and did not
participate in this debate. Some economists of nationalist persua-
sion protested but Nehru brushed them aside.

On the other hand Mahatma never had any doubt about the need
for making clear distinction between Indian and British capitalists.
In fact his approach was more general. He has said that he would
not mind Englishmen remaining in India but he wanted the elimination of institutions connected with the European and British
civilizations. What happened was exactly the opposite. White
Englishmen have gone but their places have been taken by brown
Englishmen. It may be worthwhile to mention that as long ago as
the Irwin-Gandhi Pact, the Mahatma insisted upon the insertion of
the words 'in the interests of India'. Among other things this
specifically related to the rights of Indians to picket all foreign cloth
shops. Obviously, this implied discrimination between Indian and
the British cloth manufacturers. Lord Irwin did not seem to agree.
The problem was not only of textiles but also of other industries.

The dumping of industries on the Indian economy, facilitated
first by 1949 Policy Resolution on foreign capital, was accelerated

subsequently by other industrial policy resolutions. Besides these policy resolutions the so-called science and technology policies and unlimited desire for foreign aid to which was always tied the import of a certain kind of technology, finance and some management, completed the whole gambit of a framework which resorted to the dumping of industries as a substitute for dumping of goods.

Since every developed imperial country resorted to protection, which it denied to its colonies under rule, the industrialists from the former thought it best to dump uncompetitive industries by shifting production by locating such industries in the former colonies in order to exploit the cheap raw material and labour and transmit profits back to their own countries. There were vast profits in this scheme, no matter higher were the terrif walls. The dumping of industries could be pushed under the guise of developing countries' import substitution policies. The following methods were adopted:

Dumping of industries took the open route of collaborations which seemed any easy road but was in reality leading to a precipice. The problem of foreign collaboration has a direct bearing on relationship between the Indian R&D establishments and the use of their scientific results. We know that despite hundreds of crores of rupees invested in the laboratories and scientific establishments, there are not very many inventions and discoveries to their credit even in the applied field let alone in the field of pure science. The worst part of the story is that even when inventions and discoveries are made, there is a built-in resistance to use them and this resistance comes from the culture of collaborations.

Although the culture of collaborations got fully entrenched during Mrs. Gandhi's reign, she realised although quite late as to what really was happening. However, it was the Janata Prime Minister who pointed out the nature of disease even though not much was done to change the culture. At a meeting of the Directors of national laboratories held in September, 1977 at which the major complaint made was that the results of their research were not being utilized adequately, the Prime Minister said. 'It has also been reported that some of the Ministries have, in disregard of the work of laboratories, gone in for foreign collaboration. Some of the Ministries have set up their own R&D establishments in areas in which government laboratories are functioning. There has to be proper coordination of efforts, and avoidable duplication has to be checked.'[4]

India has signed more than 15,000 collaboration agreements in both manufacturing and non-manufacturing fields. The number in former seems equal to that of all large industrial enterprises having an investment of rupees twenty crores or more. Every year now the Government issues about 1,000 licences for setting up businesses which is more or less equal to foreign collaboration agreement. Of these 1,000 licences nearly 800 apply for foreign collaborations. At the end of the year, nearly 300 licencees give up. This leaves a situation of nearly one to one correspondence between licensed industry and foreign collaboration. In recent years, not a single licensed enterprise has been set up without foreign collaboration. The paradox of the Indian industry is that the more it expands the less self-reliant it become and the potential for self-reliance remains undeveloped and unutilised.

Over four decades, penetration of foreign capital, with low level technology and high profits and remittances went on. Except for so-called Indianization of management—Indians who were easily coopted as were the ICS and others by the British imperialists without coercion—nothing was done to protect Indian interests. In the mean time, the character of the Indian bourgeoisie had undergone qualitative change from being aggressively nationalist to soft compradores.

The Foreign Exchange Regulation Act (FERA), 1973 which came into force on January 1, 1974 provided among others, the regulatory framework regarding trading, commercial and industrial activities, of branches of foreign companies in India, and Indian joint stock companies with non-resident participation of more than 40 per cent. Under Section 29 of the Act, all companies (other than banking companies) incorporated outside India and Indian companies with more than 40 per cent non-resident interest, had to obtain a fresh permission from the Reserve Bank of India to carry on business and were required to comply with the directions that might be given by the Reserve Bank on permissible level of foreign participation in the capital structure.

In general foreign investment was viewed as a vehicle for transfer of technology but the emphasis remained more an foreign equity participation (40 per cent) rather than on technology result-

[4] *Hindustan Times*, Sept. 30, 1977.

ing in import of second rate technology. Besides, the intent of importing most sophisticated technology remain on paper only, except in a few sections. When investment in technology imports did not produce desired results, equity participation condition was relaxed. A new category of companies came into existence, called FERA. The participation of foreigners further shifted the emphasis from technology and investment. In 1983 came another jolt. The foreign equity participation was allowed to be in cash and was not necessarily linked to import of machinery and equipment. In reality there was no dilution, the foreign companies simply increased their capital issue and they could attract as much as they desired. Four-fifths of imports of companies under collaborations were in the form of raw materials.

Apart from export restrictions, the foreign collaboration agreements included other restrictions in one case or another. There were no obligations with regard to supply of raw materials and plant and machinery but restrictions were placed on manufacture of products similar to those produced under the collaboration agreements. There were serious constraints relating to patents and other intellectual property rights. From 1977 onwards when the list of industries was issued in which no foreign collaboration was to be permitted, year after year condition after condition was removed even when foreign companies did not give any concession or accept restrictions. Tables at the end of the book sum up the situation.[5] What Gandhi had warned against, the Government simply fell into the trap.

The economic criteria used for measuring self-reliance in this country has been simply limited to measuring the ratio of imports to domestic production because this is the usual text book measure. Real measure is not this ratio in terms of products but ratio in terms of technologies, i.e., the ratio of the import of technology to domestic technologies in each case. If by using the former, one can show that India has become self-reliant, the situation is exactly the opposite if we use the latter criteria. The recent policy of liberalization has exposed the technological lag in Indian industries. Since the government opted for higher technology and import liberalization, they may ask and answer the question about this ratio and judge for themselves whether there is more or less self-reliance in

[5] *Foreign Collaboration in Indian Industry,* Fourth Survey Report 1985, Reserve Bank of India, Bombay.

this country. The vast expansion of FERA and pseudo-FERA companies defies all accepted criteria of self-reliance.

There were other sectors in the economy which did not need any particular import of technology or raw materials or were engaged in exports. But they were forced to compete with the 'dumped industries' whose products did not and could not compete in the global market. Hundreds of thousands of small enterprises in this country fall in this category. These enterprises tried to optimize the use of natural endowments, local resources and skills and limited markets for the low, middle income people. A proper measure of self-reliance would be the upgradation of technologies of this sector and more significantly increase in the ratio of this sector to that sector which depended on the import of technology.

In other words, we must use three criteria for self-reliance; (1) ratio of imports to domestic production in general and basic goods in particular, (2) ratio of licensed industries going for collaboration to those not going for collaboration and (3) ratio of industries depending on imported technology to those relying on domestic technology. Only then can we judge whether imported technologies, collaborating industries are or are not dumped. If all these three ratios decline together, whatever be their speed, we shall call it a trend towards self-reliance. If any of these components moves in the opposite direction, not only does it hurt self-reliance, it is said to promote dumping of industries and neocolonialism.

Protectionism has forced a particular pattern of industrialization on the LDCs. The protectionist policies may be of the ADCs or of the LDCs. The latter have deluded themselves into believing that if they are allowed to protect their industries and ADCs keep their trade doors open, every thing will turn out to their advantage. This is not true. If one looks at the percentage of protected trade of the ADCs, it is not more then 15 per cent of the total, though even this much can cripple some of the small size LDCs. The experience of the last four decades suggests that except for a handful of alert and self-conscious nations, others even while having access to ADCs markets have been less careful to fill the technological gap. Consequently their dependence on import of technologies and machines further increased as their trade expanded and they set up new industries with high import contents. The so-called policy of import substitution have led to the setting up of second-rate industries. Even when new industries were set up with latest technologies, it became a matter of time when the ADCs established their tehnol-

ogical superiority by new inventions. Because they do not indigen-
ise industries the LDCs have to wait for the import of new technologies and during this time trade advantage are appropriated by the
ADCs. Thus all kinds of gaps have evidenced: (1) The trade gap, (2)
technological gap, (3) industrialization gap and, of course, (4) the
weapons gap. The most explicit case is of the dependency of the
weapon systems and weapon industries in the LDCs.

So many third world countries made so much noise for so long
about industrial self-reliance that one would have thought that
most of them would have achieved it by now or would be on way
to achieve it. India made the loudest noises and justified her policies
of 'imported' import substitution, foreign aid, repeat of transfer
technology, export promotion and measures relating to interdependence, all in the name of self-reliance. Is India more self-reliant
than she was before? Is she more self-reliant for purposes of further
development? The answer to the first question is probably yes but
the second is a definite no.

The most important sector connected with self-reliance and
technical change is the capital goods sector because this sector is
directly involved in the process of technology generation and
diffusion of modified or new machinery and equipment. Without
building its own capital base no LDC can generally achieve self-
reliance. Another more powerful case for the capital industries is
that the technical change in these industries is always capital saving
irrespective of the labour employed, thus permitting an increasing
supply of capital. Besides, it is empirically proved in all economies
that total factor productivity tends to increase more rapidly in the
capital goods sector than in others.

The experience of Japan and South Korea have proved the truth
of this assertion, as was shown in their rapidly increasing per capita
manufacturing value added to changes in per capita GDP. Modifi-
cation, adaptation and innovation of capital equipment first occurs
in the capital goods sector and then they are diffused to other
sectors. Rosenberg has observed that a unique feature of the capital
goods sectors follows from the fact that producers of capital goods
are often at the same time users of some of the machines that they
produce. Consequently, user-producer information and technological flows are internalised within the firm thus making it possible for more efficient flows of information in countries which rely
on impact of technology and do not have their own capital base.
Information from producers to users is limited and users to produc-

ers is non-existent. There is ample evidence to prove that the capital goods produced by the LDCs are quite different from those that are available from the ADCs.

By ignoring the building of their adequate capital base industries and by importing second rate technologies and industries the LDCs have created a double industrial and technological gap; (1) between the technology of its industrial sector and that of the developed countries with which it desires to compete in the international market and (2) between the respective technologies of its own industrial and rural sectors. The former gap has not narrowed despite massive import substitution, technology transfer, creation of scientific know-how and know-why, etc. largely because the rate of technological growth in the developed world has been much faster. The second gap has also widened because except for patches of Green Revolution, agricultural technology has remained more or less old fashioned. Now a very important point emerges. If now, rather late in the day, dominant strategy of development is to be export promotion, then it will, under the existing economic struc-ture, lead to putting most of new technological and investment resources in specific industrial sector. Once again the old experi-ence may be repeated. ADCs technologies which moved forward faster and are more productive will increase the time lag in our adapting to resource endowment, thereby increasing the vast gap even further. Sooner or later, just as the import substitution ended up in a crisis in the mid-sixties, excessive reliance on the export substitution strategy too may end up in a crisis. It must be remembered that despite substantial expansion of exports during the last few years, the non-export sector, i.e., most of the economy, still operates at a low level, if not in stagnation. Besides, during the phase of export promotion, the second technological gap would have further widened. There is thus no hope with this new strategy when adopted in isolation.

Stock of knowledge and the creation of knowledge go together with technological development. In the dual enclave economies of the LDCs both knowledge and technology remain confined to one small area without any diffusion or permeation to the other. Crea-tion of production with knowledge and technology remained absent.

Most LDCs have had no system of research priorities. The imperial powers have constrained them from conceptualizing the relevant technical change. Their post-Independent tie-up with the education system, particularly the technical education system and the collaboration agreements for import of technology, have had their set priorities put there by others. Let alone other countries even India cannot claim to have, after 40 years of development, possible directions of future research. The tragedy is that during the Nehru era India had a science policy but no technology policy. In the post-Nehru era, she had a technology policy but no science policy. In the last 10 years it is either both or neither, and documents on science and technology remain irrelevant to one another as well as to the process of change at the level of firms. International circumstances keep their weight and intervene.

The debate in the LDCs which missed the point that neither neo-classical economics had an adequate theory of technical change nor the public sector claiming to have commanding heights had a serious technological content other than what was imported from abroad. The scientific and technological laborataries and institutions served neither the public sector nor the private sector firms as they remained there supplying in isolation. Thus LDCs like India remained technologically dormant as they never attempted fundamental reconceptualisation of the nature of their technological needs independent of what was available from outside. Even for paradigms they did not have enough empirical studies to make their own. Besides policies on pricing, production, etc. were conceived without any relationship with technological development.

Right from the beginning an assumption was made that change is instantaneous and non-problematic and once technology was available from outside, things would move on a linear fashion. But even the organisational structures needed to assimilate imported technology were given scant attention. It is not therefore surprising that the degree of diffusion of selected technologies remained weak. The state which was to shape the entire technological knowledge confined its activities to creating scientific and technological institutions and yet kept them away from being used by firms. Even exporters did not know what technology was being produced in the country to give them competitive strength.

India is a tragic example of a nation which claims to have created vast among scientific manpower which is redundant within the context of global knowledge order. Indian educational and scientific institutions are imitators rather than producers of knowledge. There is overinvestment, repeated imitation and abysmally low underinvestment in productionof knowledge. At best the whole system relies on incremental addition to imported knowledge. Expansion and diversification of industries are based on imitation, repetition of imports and incremental technological improvement. The more the industry expands the greater is the technological gap—the double gap—between ADCs and LDCs and different industrial sectors within LDCs.

A Gandhian response to this terribly blocked situation on the industrial sector will be the following:

(a) Except for very very selective cases, there should be no foreign collaboration. Whatever technologies are needed must be purchased in the market even if it means paying a much higher price.

(b) The same principle would apply to foreign capital as in the long-run it would be far more beneficial to pay higher price for capital borrowing than agreeing to many explicit and implicit strings attached to low-interest borrowing from World Bank and other international financial institutions.

(c) There would be no repeated import of the same technologies or even new technologies for the same products without showing that domestic R&D has not been successful for reasons beyond control.

(d) Industries producing mass consumption goods will neither have foreign capital nor import technology of any kind if it is labour displacing.

(e) Diversification of industries must not lead to diversification of dependence. If more and more industries come under FERA collaboration, dependency will increase. Industries must rely on one another on indigenous items and technologies.

(f) Industrial and technological manpower planning should not be considered in terms of third hand extrapolation of current deadening trends of second rate technologies.

(g) Gandhi did not and probably could not anticipate all the reasons we know now are responsible for the inappropriateness of the technology transfer from the developed to the LDC countries. But surprisingly or rather not so surprisingly, the results and conclusions from empirical analysis are the same as Gandhi's, a priori analysis. What lies behind this similarity? In most non-Gandhian analysis, unemployment and low incomes correlation, while accepted in theory, was left out in arriving at choices of techniques. Gandhi never separated them. Therefore, the consequences of choices in technology and transfer of technology starting with the aim of generating growth of income, heavily impinged on employment. Gandhi did not have to go through these exercise as he saw the same happening in the most perverse way as a result of British imperialist economic policies as applied to India.

(h) Gandhian approach to technology is not to allow the creation of any dualism, which has become the hallmark of many LDC economies. Since developed countries's technology is associated with high rates of productivity, it must be reflected, under capitalism in high wages or profits, if no other serious bottlenecks are there. Now if the diffusion of such a technology is limited, it creates dangerous dualism which Gandhi clearly saw occurring during the British rule The dualism can be filled or sustained by the dumping of industries. The reason why he was against the import of foisted technologies through aid was that any increase in wages and profits in the so-called urban sector which left others particularly rural workers wages depressed was not acceptable to him. The results of the experience of the LDCs over the last four decades are the same what Gandhi arrived at from a limited experience.

(i) During Gandhi's days, information and communication revolutions were decades afar. No matter how much one wants to isolate oneself, one just cannot do so. Radio and microwaves, satellites, televisions, the lasers, the chips and computers are at outdoor steps. The creation of these technologies is knowledge and science based and if not monopolized can be materialized for use in small societies. The LDCs must make an effort to adopt big technologies into small ones with the help of science. Less dependence on trade and minimization of foreign collaboration do not mean ignoring science and technology based information system.

CONCLUSION

All the crises, dialectics and paradoxes stated in the preceding chapters do not explain the reality fully. In the final analysis, the style of life of the ruling elites of the LDCs stands between the present global disorder and the liberation of the people of the South from that disorder. Generally, it is the lifestyle that determines the quality that a political system acquires as emerging from the economic system. The irony of the situation in the LDCs is that their ruling elites have been trying to imitate the lifestyles of the ADCs and of classes which have been once attacked as the expression of exploitation of the colonial people. Indeed, there is a double irony. The same instrument of ideology and class consciousness which were important inputs in the national independence movement became precisely the instruments of domestic oppression and external dependence. Country after country, when former colonies became independent, turned culturally and ideologically more and more dependent until they reached the present situation of international Darwinism. The political elite to whom the power was transferred found it easier to rule their respective peoples by getting coopted or by coopting the administrative and constitutional system left behind by the colonial rulers. The most obvious example is that of the Indian Civil Service (ICS) being coopted by Jawaharlal Nehru and his Congress Party. It did not occur to him that the class of bureaucrats who till the night before independence were denounced as agents of British imperialism could not become, the very next day, instruments of social and economic transformation. Moreover, instead of bridging the social and economic gulf between themselves and the masses by adopting austerity, accountability, honesty etc., the political elites were lured into the western style of living which compelled them to resort to crude exploitation and exhibit the most arrogant selfishness largely because the economic base of the society was too narrowly held for another kind of distribution. In turn, the rise of a permissive society and consumerism undermined the bases of rapid growth and social justice by imposing new inequalities on the old ones.

The most critical role played in this transformation was that of the education system which was lock, stock and barrel an imitation of the ADC system and a continuation of the well-structured colonial system. Thereby the children of the ruling elites were further encouraged to adopt their parents' style of life. Even the language of the colonial masters became the language of the new educational, administrative and communication system. Consequently, the ruling elites became more and more dependent and parasitic as they got integrated with the ADCs and still more and more alienated from their own masses. It became easier for them to legitimize their position because they successfully sold to their people western modes of thinking, models of development, ideologies and cultural patterns of life. Instead of thinking for themselves, they let the old masters think for them and provide them with the vital justification of pursuing the same course of development as the ADCs did. The LDCs have been imitators and that too very bad ones, rather than producers of knowledge.

But the transplant withered except that it left behind a style of life from which there was no escape. The attempt to establish autonomy on the very ground of dependence became both a farce and a tragedy. Most significantly, corruption and rank opportunism became the most important instruments for sustaining the ruling elites of the LDCs and maintaining their lifestyles. Corruption became so rampant that the entire process of upward social mobility became subject to its compulsions than to merit, efficiency and accountability. One man's vulgarity was another man's misery.

Mahatma Gandhi had insisted upon the code of conduct and style of life of the leaders of the national movement in order that they did not get alienated from the masses. In fact, he was so conscious of and careful about the lifestyles of the leaders and political workers trained by him that he almost made it an active part of the cultural resistance to British imperialism. His approach was hailed by the leaders of the other third world countries struggling for independence. But like his Indian successors, they too forgot the message and their earlier commitment. He made no bones about the imperative of a trade-off between power and affluence. A nation's position on one scale determines its position on the other scale—the sensitivity of those who have wealth or power or both. Leaders who controlled political power had to set examples of austerity and honesty in order to convince the masses of the need for sacrifice in order to have rapid growth with justice. He wanted them to transform all symbols of imperialism into instruments of service. Unfortunately, his successors did just the opposite. They followed the whole of the colonial pattern of administration, education, lifestyles, etc.

Gandhi also made it very clear that without spiritual and moral development there could be no true economic development. For him, the first principle of economics was provision of basic needs though not without corresponding obligations. He defined his system as that of Moral Political Economy, a concept which some economists are now beginning to grapple with. He openly declared that there could be no flight from poverty to spirituality. Poverty was a curse except when it was voluntary and which in turn implied austerity and transcendence. Gandhi was distorted by his detractors by their saying that he glorified poverty. He openly stated that whether it is poverty or affluence, it has to be distributed on moral grounds. For development there has to be equal sacrifice. The distance between the masses and the leaders had to be minimized. This had a very clear meaning for the style of life of the rulers. His successors neglected this approach totally and that is why we are reaping the poisoned harvest of a generation of demagogues, pseudo-modernist, ineffectual and parasitic leaders.

The crux of the problem is that the integration of the ruling elites of the LDCs with those of the ADCs, which was justified as an instrument of global integration and the creation of an international community, has precisely produced opposite results for the LDCs, i.e., economic rupture. The idea of one world has became a nightmare for the masses of the LDCs as the gap between the LDCs and ADCs widened in terms of all parameters discussed in the earlier chapter. The LDC power elite's self-rightousness and narcissism are matched by their anxiety to push as quietly as possible towards globalization. We have already shown that in place of one world there is a global economic disruption precisely because of the widening gulf between the ADCs and LDCs. At the centre of it all lies the lifestyle of the ruling elites of the latter who are caught in a crisis of irrelevance while their nations are teetering on the brink of economic collapse. It became the greatest paradox of our times that in the LDCs things became worse as they seemed to get better.

Even more important is the total insensitivity and irresponsibility of the ruling elites, their lacking in all moral and historical perspectives. In fact, although like the ADCs, the LDCs have rulers and the ruled, but no ruling class, though not in the Marxist sense. No country can seriously progress or even survive in independence without a self-conscious ruling class which, after taking whatever share of the GDP it thinks necessary or appropriate, transcends both its interest and alienation and identifies itself with the rest of the nation. It is tragic that countries like India which have a civilizational character should have missed the point that without evolving such a ruling class which is also conscious of its civilizational heritage, they could not maintain their autonomy or identity and membership of the global order. That is why whereas their rulers fought in the name of democracy most of them ultimately degenerated into dictatorships of the worst kind. It is not surprising that the rulers of authoritarian regimes are more dependent on the ADCs, and have the most vulgar lifestyle. The ADCs supported them and it was this support or connivance that led Russell to say that the western civilization offered the LDCs a 'firm foundation of despair'.

Lifestyles are not autonomously decided. They are consequences of internal and external economic policies. The irony is that in both the successive phases, of import substitution and trade promotion, the attitude to lifestyles did not change because both phases were marked by external economic dependence. In their anxiety to get out of their accumulated crises and maintain their power and lifestyles, the rulers of the LDCs are further pushing their countries towards globalization without realizing that trade is a double-edged weapon. Trade can promote development but trade dependency can retard development and retarded development, in turn, leads to ever-increasing trade dependency.

Throughout recorded history, there have been periods when the people sought to exchange their high style of life based on property, social hierarchy and archaic institutions for more humane ways to live. The power elite in the LDCs have blocked this exchange and thus become more and more parasitic. By becoming loathsomely vulgar and contemptuous of their own people, the power elite have reduced themselves to being no more than historical onlookers. But history plays tricks on those who try to bend or mould it for narrow sectarian interests. That is what is happening in the LDCs. Paradoxically, in their diminished mode of consciousness, the proponents of globalism, be they of the Dependency or Interdependence school, are being self-alienated and self-Darwinized. Their lifestyles and worship of consumerism cannot provide them with the necessary psychic leverage to lift their nations from the wasteland of Darwinism. The answer lies in a new cultural revolution and resistance among the people of the South because it is through the fatal paradox of cultural imperialism that the world is becoming so knit as to Darwinize the LDCs.

TABLE I

World Trade Imports and Exports

(Billions of dollars)

		IMPORT								EXPORT							
		1950	1955	1960	1965	1970	1975	1980	1985	1950	1955	1960	1965	1970	1975	1980	1985
I. 1.	World	63	97	135	197	329	982	2054	2043	61	93	128	187	314	874	1988	1939
II.	Developed Market Economies	41	65	89	137	238	614	1406	1386	37	60	86	129	225	579	1270	1265
III.	Developing Market Economies	17	24	29	37	56	186	463	437	19	24	27	36	56	200	540	470
(a)	The Gang of Four*			1	2	5	17	44	71			1	1	4	15	40	8
(b)	O.P.E.C.	2	4	5	6	10	52	122	120	4	6	8	11	18	113	296	15
(c)	Least Developed Countries	1	1	1	2	2	7	16	14	1	1	1	2	2	3	6	6
IV.	Centrally Planned Economies	5	9	17	23	35	102	185	217	5	9	15	22	33	86	177	203

U.N: *International Trade Strategies Year Book, 1980 and 1985 Far Eastern Economic Review Annual 1987.*

* Korea, Taiwan, Honkong and Singapore.

TABLE II

Indicators of International Technology Flows, 1962-85

(Billions of dollars, current prices)

Indicator	1962	1972	1973	1974	1975	1976	1977	1978	1979	1980	1981	1982	1983	1984	1985
FOREIGN DIRECT INVESTMENT															
1. Flows from ADCs to world of which	4.7	14.5	24.0	23.1	27.2	27.0	27.5	37.7	58.3	53.5	50.6	23.4	31.8	40.0	57.2
2. Other ADCs.	2.8	9.2	13.4	20.6	14.5	13.7	18.6	24.7	32.8	41.2	42.2	30.1	33.6	39.9	33.7
3. Flows From ADCs to LDCs	1.4	4.4	6.7	6.6	10.5	7.8	9.5	11.1	13.5	10.1	15.3	10.4	7.8	11.3	7.7
RECEIPTS OF ROYALTIES AND FEES															
4. Flows to ADCs	–	3.9	4.5	5.4	5.9	6.4	7.2	8.2	8.8	9.9	11.1	11.2	12.1	–	–
5. Flows from LDCs	–	0.7	0.7	0.9	1.0	1.0	1.1	1.5	1.7	2.0	2.2	2.0	2.3	2.2	2.3
TECHNICAL ASSISTANCE															
6. Flows to LDCs.	0.7	1.8	2.3	2.5	2.2	2.9	3.1	3.8	4.7	5.5	5.2	5.4	5.8	5.9	6.0
MEMO ITEM:															
Export unit values of manufacturers (1980 = 100)	29.5	39.3	46.3	55.8	63.3	63.0	69.9	79.3	90.0	100.0	94.8	91.5	88.5	85.0	85.7

ADCs = Advanced Developed Countries   LDCs = Less Developed Countries

Source: UNCTAD Annual Report 1986

TABLE III

Developing Countries' Share of Manufacturing Value-Added

Year	Total LDCs Share	Total LDCs ann.%	NICs Share	NICs ann.%	Other LDCs Share	Other LDCs ann.%
1938	10.4%	–	4.4	–	6.0	
1948	14.0	+3.5	4.9	+1.1	9.1	+1.2
1966	12.2	–0.7	5.9	+1.1	6.3	–1.7
1973	14.0	+2.1	7.1	+2.9	6.9	+1.4
1979	14.8	+0.7	8.1	+3.3	6.1	–1.9
1984	13.9	–1.0	8.4	–0.2	5.5	–2.0

Source: *New Left Review*, June 1988

TABLE IV

Growth in Volume of Developing Countries' Industrial Production

Periods	Total LDCs Ave. ann%	NICs Ave. ann%
1948-1966	9.4	14.4
1966-1973	10.7	13.0
1973-1979	4.7	7.8
1979-1984	0.9	1.8

Source: *New Left Review*, June 1988

TABLE V

SURVEY OF FOREIGN COLLABORATION
Industry-wise Classification of Agreements with Export
Restrictions (1977–81)

Industry	Subsidiaries		Minority capital participation		Technical collaboration		Total	
	No. of agreements		No. of agreements		No. of agreements		No. of agreements	
	With export restrictions	Total	With export restrictions	Total	With export restrictions	Total	With export restrictions	Total
	1	2	3	4	5	6	7	8
I. Plantations and mining	—	—	1	2	—	—	1	2
II. Petroleum	—	—	—	1	—	—	—	1
III. Manufacturing	29	48	163	283	154	224	346	555
Foods, beverages & tobacco	—	—	—	3	2	3	2	6
Textile Products	—	—	1	6	2	3	3	9
Transport equipment	1	1	12	19	17	21	30	41
Machinery & machine tools	2	7	62	85	87	118	151	210
Metals and metal products	2	5	10	24	10	22	22	51
Electrical machinery and apparatus	17	21	44	57	19	27	80	105
Chemicals and chemical products	7	14	21	67	13	22	41	103
(i) Basic industrial	2	4	9	46	6	14	17	64
(ii) Drugs & medicines	4	8	6	10	3	3	13	21
(iii) Others	1	2	6	11	4	5	11	18
Rubber products	—	—	5	8	2	4	7	12
Miscellaneous	—	—	8	14	2	4	10	18
IV. Services	—	1	4	14	3	7	7	22
Total (I+II+III+IV)	29	49	168	300	157	231	354	580

Source: *Foreign Collaborations in Indian Industry,*
Fourth Survey Report 1985,
Reserve Bank of India, Bombay.
(Page 46)

TABLE VI
Details Regarding Types of Regulatory Clauses (1977–81)

Type of regulatory clauses	No. of clauses			
	Subsidiaries	Minority capital participation	Technical collaboration	Total (1+2+3)
	1	2	3	4
I. Export clauses Of which:				
(i) Total ban on exports	—	—	3	3
(ii) Prohibition of exports to countries in which the collaborator operates through branches/ subsidiaries/affiliates or is having similar collaboration agreements	12	115	125	252
(iii) Prohibition of exports to collaborator's country	3	53	90	146
(iv) Prohibition of exports to countries other than those covered in (ii) and (iii) above	6	8	33	47
(v) Permission of collaborator for exports is needed	7	43	30	80
(vi) Exports only through collaborator/his agents/ distributors	1	6	7	14

Source: *Foreign Collaboration in Indian Industry*,
Fourth Survey Report 1985,
Reserve Bank of India, Bombay.
(Page 47)